UNDERSTANDING VARIATION

THE KEY TO MANAGING CHAOS

SECOND EDITION

DONALD J. WHEELER

SPC Press

Overhead Transparencies for this book are available from SPC Press.

Copies of this book may be obtained directly from SPC Press.

SPC Press
5908 Toole Drive, Suite C
Knoxville, Tennessee 37919
(865) 584-5005
Fax (865) 588-9440
(800) 545-8602
www.spcpress.com

ISBN 0 - 945320 - 53 - 1
x + 158 pages
116 figures

17 18 19 20 21 22 23 24 25 26 27 28 29 30

Dust Jacket Photograph:
Messier 27 in *Vulpecula*
photographed with the Hale 200-inch telescope
Mt. Palomar Observatory
Copyright © 1961 California Institute of Technology and
Carnegie Institution of Washington
Used with permission

CONTENTS

INTRODUCTION

We live in the "Information Age," and much of that information comes to us in the form of numbers. Indeed, wherever we look we are surrounded by ever increasing mountains of data—indexes and polls, market reports and leading indicators, government reports, balances of this and imbalances of that, data showing that food causes cancer and cancer cures smoking.

Yet, in spite of the increase in databases and spreadsheets, in spite of the speed with which one can be tied into networks to access, tally, and report data, we are told that our productivity is falling, our manufacturing base is eroding, and our economy is getting weaker. While we have faster and larger number crunching machines, and increasing access to these machines, and while we are making great strides in many areas of basic science, we are told that our technological edge is slipping and that others are taking the lead in transferring scientific knowledge into applied products for society's use.

Closer to home, businessmen are finding that while they have more numbers than ever before, they still do not know what these numbers mean. If the numbers changed for the better compared to last month, then just wait—they will change for the worse soon enough. If the numbers actually changed for the worse compared to last month, then the apocalypse is at hand and all are doomed! The boss is in despair—"Don't just stand there, do something!" You have to come up with an explanation of why the numbers were so bad, or else find a scapegoat, by 10:30 tomorrow morning. Moreover—how are you going to keep these bad numbers from happening again? How are you going to get the workers to work harder? "And Pharaoh said, 'You are lazy! You will be given no straw, but you must produce the same tally of bricks each day.'" And so it goes, month after month, world without end. From the dawn of time until the present, there is nothing new under the sun—just more of it.

The problem with our information age was succinctly stated by Daniel Boorstin when he said: "Information is random and miscellaneous, but knowledge is orderly and cumulative." Before information can be useful it must be analyzed, interpreted, and assimilated. In short, raw data have to be digested before they can be useful.

This process of digesting data has been widely neglected at all levels of our educational system. Managers and workers, educators and students, accountants and businessmen, financial analysts and bankers, doctors and nurses, and especially lawyers and journalists all have one thing in common. They come out of their educational experience knowing how to add, subtract, multiply, and divide, *yet they have no understanding of how to digest numbers to extract the knowledge that may be locked up inside the data.* In fact, this shortcoming is also seen, to a lesser extent, among engineers and scientists.

This deficiency has been called "numerical naiveté." Numerical naiveté is not a failure with arithmetic, but it is instead a failure to know how to use the basic tools of arithmetic to understand data. Numerical naiveté is not addressed by the traditional courses in the primary or secondary schools, nor is it addressed by advanced courses in mathematics. *This is why even highly educated individuals can be numerically naive.*

Fortunately, the cure for numerical naiveté is very simple. The principles are easy to grasp and the techniques are very easy to implement. This book was written to help organizations overcome the effects of numerical naiveté.

The use of the techniques presented in this book can have profound consequences both for individuals and for organizations. These techniques have been thoroughly proven in over 70 years of practice in all walks of life. However, until these techniques are actually put into use nothing will happen. Numerical naiveté can only be overcome through practice. This book will tell you how to go about it. The real world will give you the opportunities for practice.

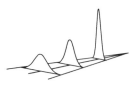

ACKNOWLEDGMENTS

I would like to thank those who have helped and encouraged me in bringing this book to completion. First among these are Sheila Poling and Frances Wheeler who faithfully read and re-read the material, catching mistakes, making suggestions, and asking for clarifications at those points where the prose was obscure. Other readers include Frony Ward and Wade Meyercord. In addition, there is Steve Cobb who encouraged me to begin this work, and Tom Sands and Bob Kasprzyk who made many helpful suggestions in the early drafts. Finally, there is Bob Lucke who kindly checked all of the computations. The contributions of these individuals have made this book a better book.

PREFACE TO THE SECOND EDITION

This edition includes three new appendices and an index that were not in the original version. In addition I have taken this opportunity to update the nomenclature throughout the book. The original version used the traditional labels which have been used during the past 50 years. However, since this book is about the nontraditional applications of the process behavior chart to managerial and administrative data, it is appropriate to use words that are more descriptive of what is intended. Therefore throughout this book the following changes in wording have been made:

"Control charts" have become "process behavior charts."

An "in-control process" has become a "predictable process."

An "out-of-control process" has become an "unpredictable process."

An "out-of-control point" has become a "point outside the limit."

An "in-control point" has become a "point inside the limits."

And variation is described as being either "routine" or "exceptional." Thus, jargon has been replaced by ordinary words and phrases having the intended connotation.

The intent of these changes is to remove the barriers of inappropriate terminology, and thereby to make this powerful approach more accessible to those who are not familiar with the traditional jargon.

Those readers who would like more information about the rationale for this change in nomenclature will find the appendix titled "A Modest Proposal" to be of interest.

May 1999

ONE

DATA ARE RANDOM
AND MISCELLANEOUS

Recently the U.S. Trade Balance for February showed a deficit of 11.4 billion dollars. As a descriptive value, this deficit means that the U.S. imported goods worth 11.4 billion dollars more than it exported during this particular month. Clearly, a trade balance deficit of this size is bad, but what does it mean about the larger picture? Are things getting better or worse? Comparisons are needed in order to make sense of this number.

For example, this deficit for February was 1.4 billion *larger* than the deficit for January of the same year. This comparison would suggest that things are getting worse—beware!

However, the February deficit of 11.4 billion was 1.6 billion *smaller* than the deficit for February of the previous year. This comparison would suggest that things are getting better!

In an election year you would undoubtedly hear both comparisons being made, leading to the old conclusion that there are "lies, damn lies, and statistics!"

The problem with both of the comparisons above is their limited nature. While it is good to try and place the single value for February in some larger context, and while both of the comparisons above are correct, neither is conclusive. No comparison between two values can be global. A simple comparison between the current figure and some previous value cannot fully capture and convey the behavior of any time series. Yet comparisons of the current value with another value are the most common type of comparisons encountered.

For example, virtually all government figures are subjected to this type of comparison when they are reported in the press. The figure for this month is compared to the value from the preceding month. If this month's value has changed for the better, things are looking up. If this month's value has changed for the worse, watch out!

In a similar vein, automobile sales are tallied and reported every 10 days. These values are always compared to the sales figures for the same 10-day period from the previous year. Do you remember how sales were doing during this 10-day period last year? Of course you don't! So just what is the basis for making such a comparison? Why would this comparison provide additional insight into the current sales figures? Comparisons of this sort are built on the implicit assumption that last year was normal. You do recall how normal last year was, don't you?

And if we tend to take business data at face value, we do it even more readily with sports data. Consider the record for the number of home runs in a single season. This category, like virtually all sports categories, is an arbitrary one, selected for no other reason than to create a "record" and a "record holder." For many years the record holder was Roger Maris, who hit 61 home runs in the 1961 season.[1] Next came Babe Ruth with a record of 60 home runs in the 1927 season. From 1961 to 1990 there was an asterisk next to Roger's record. This asterisk represented a footnote that commented upon the fact that Roger Maris' record season was longer than the season in which Babe Ruth set his record. So what was the purpose of the asterisk? It attempted to provide some contextual information which would modify the interpretation of the raw data. Such as it was, this information was perfectly appropriate. However, since it was an exception to the usual way of presenting such records, the asterisk was removed in 1990, thereby proving that business holds no monopoly on numerical naiveté.

---

[1] Obviously this book was written before the 1998 season when Mark McGwire and Sammy Sosa both surpassed Roger's record.

Finally, think about the traditional way in which business data are packaged in the monthly reports—several pages of tables of numbers, obtained from computer printouts, and reduced down to a size that no one over 45 can read without their bifocals. A typical monthly report might look like the one shown in Figure 1.1.

Monthly Report for July

Quality:	Dept	July Actual Value	Monthly Average Value	% Diff	% Diff from July Last Year	Year-to-Date Values: Actual Value	Year-to-Date Values: Plan or Average	% Diff	This YTD as % Diff. of Last YTD
On-Time Shipments (%)	20	91.0	91.3	− 0.3	− 0.9	90.8	91.3	− 0.6	− 0.3
First Time Approval (%)	12	54	70	− 23.0	− 10.0	69.3	70	− 1.0	− 0.4
Pounds Scrapped (per 1000 lbs production)	19	124	129	− 3.9	0.0	132	129	+ 2.3	+ 1.5

Production:	Dept	July Actual Value	Monthly Plan Value	% Diff	% Diff from July Last Year	Year-to-Date Values: Total or Average	Year-to-Date Values: Plan	% Diff	This YTD as % Diff. of Last YTD
Production Volume (1000's lbs)	13	34.5	36.	− 4.2	− 2.0	251.5	252	− 0.2	− 8.0
Material Costs ($/100 lbs)	13	198.29	201.22	− 1.5	− 1.9	198.46	201.22	− 1.4	− 3.6
Manhours per 100 lbs	13	4.45	4.16	+ 7.0	+ 4.5	4.46	4.16	+ 7.2	+ 9.3
Energy & Fixed Costs / 100 lbs	13	11.34	11.27	+ 0.6	+ 11.3	11.02	11.27	− 2.2	+ 9.2
Total Production Costs/100 lbs	13	280.83	278.82	+ 0.7	+ 0.9	280.82	278.82	+ 0.7	+ 0.4
In-Process Inventory (100's lbs)	17	28	19.7	+ 42.0	+ 12.0	21.6	19.7	+ 9.6	+ 5.9

Figure 1.1: A Typical Monthly Management Report

For each line, this monthly report:
(1) gives the current value,
(2) lists a plan or average value,
(3) compares the current value to this plan or average value,
(4) compares the current value to the value for the same month last year,
(5) gives the current year-to-date value,
(6) compares this year-to-date value with a plan or average value, and
(7) compares the current and previous year-to-date values.

The four comparisons in this list are the ones most commonly used. Collectively they try to provide some sort of context for interpreting the current values. However, since each of these four comparisons is limited, they may provide contradictory messages.

Figure 1.2: The World According to the Monthly Report

In the words of Myron Tribus:

> *"Managing a company by means of the monthly report*
> *is like trying to drive a car*
> *by watching the yellow line*
> *in the rear-view mirror."*

Nevertheless, managers use these monthly reports to run the company. Explanations are required for any figures which are not as good as they "should" be. Reports have to be written. Action plans for dealing with the problem values have to be outlined, and then the values had better improve—whatever that means!

All of the preceding examples show a common urge to provide some contextual background for the interpretation of any given number. This urge is proper and correct—you simply cannot make sense of any number without a contextual basis. Yet the traditional attempts to provide this contextual basis are often flawed in their execution. The most common of these flaws is that of a limited comparison.

PRESENTING DATA IN CONTEXT

While it is simple and easy to compare one number with another number, such comparisons are limited and weak. They are limited because of the amount of data used, and they are weak because both of the numbers are subject to the variation that is inevitably present in real world data. Since both the current value and the earlier value are subject to this variation, it will always be difficult to determine just how much of the difference between the values is due to variation in the numbers, and how much, if any, of the difference is due to real changes in the process.

It is this author's hunch that the year-to-date figures were first added to the monthly report by someone who got tired of having to explain the up and down movement of the comparison between monthly values. The year-to-date values will, as the year progresses, show less variation than the monthly values. While this will make comparisons based upon the year-to-date values easier to interpret, such comparisons are still limited in scope because they do not use the past data in an efficient manner.

Well, if limited comparisons are not enough, then how about simply presenting all of the values in a table? While this is useful, it is not enough to provide a complete analysis.

	Jan	Feb	Mar	Apr	May	Jun	Jul	Aug	Sep	Oct	Nov	Dec
1987	10.7	13.0	11.4	11.5	12.5	14.1	14.8	14.1	12.6	16.0	11.7	10.6
1988	10.0	11.4	7.9	9.5	8.0	11.8	10.5	11.2	9.2	10.1	10.4	10.5

Figure 1.3: Monthly U.S. Trade Deficits, 1987-1988 ($ billions)

While tables of values may be used to present all of the relevant data, they are not easy to summarize. It is difficult to digest the information contained in tables of numbers. Moreover, that which is not easily assimilated is generally hard to communicate to others. The human mind just does not do a very good job of absorbing large amounts of data.

Babe Ruth season	'18	'19	'20	'21	'22	'23	'24	'25	'26	'27	'28	'29	'30	'31	'32	'33	'34
home runs	11	29	54	59	35	41	46	25	47	60	54	46	49	46	41	34	22

Roger Maris season	'57	'58	'59	'60	'61	'62	'63	'64	'65	'66	'67	'68
home runs	14	28	16	39	61	33	23	26	8	13	9	5

Figure 1.4: Home Runs by Season

Thus, the traditional ways of communicating with numbers—limited comparisons and tables of data—both have severe drawbacks. The usual comparisons are narrowly focused and weak, while tables present an abundance of extraneous details.

The solution to these problems lies in a shift from a digital representation of data to a form that is more friendly to humans—graphs.

Graphs can remove the extraneous details given by tables of numbers while they focus on the interesting bits of information which may be contained within the data. Graphs provide the context for interpreting the current value because they include all of the relevant previous values, but they do this in a *visual* manner rather than in a *digital* manner which makes the information easier to assimilate.

There are two basic graphs which have proven their worth in this respect—the time series graph and the tally plot.

TIME SERIES GRAPHS

Time series graphs (or *running records*) typically have months (or years) marked off on the horizontal axis and possible values marked off on the vertical axis. As you move from left to right there is a passage of time.

Changes in the time series are seen as you scan the graph from the left to the right. By visually comparing the current value with the plotted values for the preceding months you can quickly see if the current value is unusual or not.

The time series graph for the U.S. Trade Deficit in 1987 and 1988 is shown in Figure 1.5. The graph in Figure 1.5 suggests that, compared with 1987, there might have been a slight improvement in 1988.

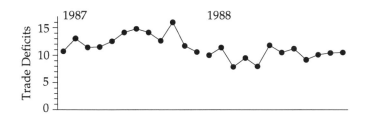

Figure 1.5: Monthly U.S. Trade Deficits 1987-1988

The time series graph for the home runs per season for both Babe Ruth and Roger Maris are shown in Figure 1.6. These graphs show the records of 60 and 61 home runs in the context of the careers of these two baseball players. Time series plots communicate the content of a data set more quickly and completely than do tables of values.

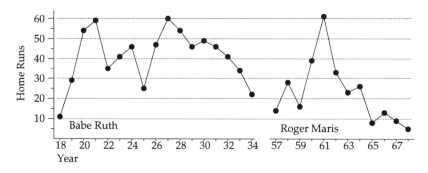

Figure 1.6: Home Run Time Series

TALLY PLOTS

A *tally plot* (or *histogram*) is simply an accumulation of the different values as they occur without trying to display the time order sequence. A mark is placed beside a possible value each time that value is observed in the sequence. If the possible values are written on the horizontal axis, then the vertical axis will represent the frequencies for the different values observed. A simple tally plot of the number of home runs per season for Babe Ruth and Roger Maris is shown in Figure 1.7.

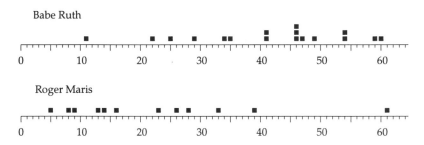

Figure 1.7: Histograms, or Tally Plots, of Home Runs Per Season

The tally plots compress the data shown on the time series. In this case the compression makes the side-by-side comparison clearer. Babe Ruth's 60 home run season was simply the high point of an outstanding career. Roger Maris' 61 home run season was, by any measure, exceptional. Still, Roger did hit 61 home runs in 1961. But should this be attributed solely to his personal skills? This question can only be answered by considering an even broader context.

COMPARING TIME SERIES

Additional insight may sometimes be gained by using two time series graphs together. Figure 1.8 shows the home runs per season for both Roger Maris and Mickey Mantle.

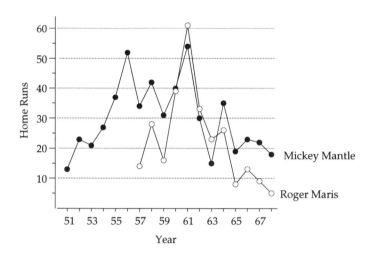

Figure 1.8: Home Runs for Roger Maris and Mickey Mantle

Roger Maris and Mickey Mantle were teammates from 1960 to 1966. The way these two running records move up and down together suggests that the number of home runs hit by each was subject to some external influence. One possible explanation is that they faced essentially the same set of pitchers each season. Perhaps the number of home runs hit by these two sluggers went up and down as the quality of the pitching staff varied from year to year.

Whatever the reason for this parallelism, the values are better understood when they are placed in a broader context.

NUMERICAL SUMMARIES OF DATA: AVERAGES

In addition to time series graphs and tally plots, it is occasionally useful to compute numerical summaries of a set of data. Of course the basic numerical summary is the arithmetic average. This average is simply the sum of the values divided by the number of values. A generic symbol for the average of a set of values will be:

$$\bar{X}$$

This symbol is commonly read as "X-bar."

The average is said to be a *measure of the location* of the set of values. Babe Ruth averaged 41.1 home runs per season between 1918 and 1934. Roger Maris averaged 22.9 home runs per season between 1957 and 1968. And Mickey Mantle averaged 29.7 home runs per season between 1951 and 1968.

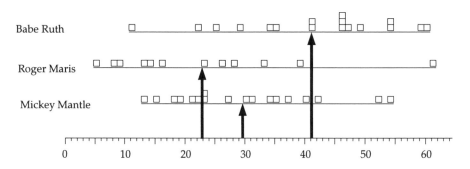

Figure 1.9: Averages for Three Histograms

Since the average is a measure of location, it is common to use averages to compare two data sets. The set with the greater average is thought to "exceed" the other set. While such comparisons may be helpful, they must be used with caution. After all, for any given data set, most of the values will *not* be equal to the average.

NUMERICAL SUMMARIES OF DATA: RANGES

A *measure of the dispersion* of a set of values is the range. The range is defined as the maximum value minus the minimum value. The generic symbol for the range is:

$$R$$

The range of the number of home runs per season for Babe Ruth is $R = 49$ for these 17 seasons. The range of the number of home runs per season for Roger Maris is $R = 56$ for these 12 seasons. The range for Mickey Mantle's 18 seasons is $R = 41$. (Here the range does little besides remind the reader that the numbers of home runs per season did deviate from the average.)

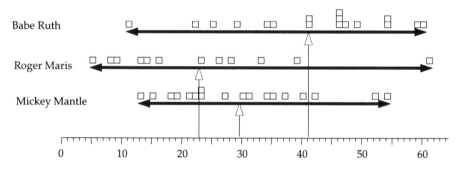

Figure 1.10: Ranges for Three Histograms

While other measures of location and dispersion exist, the average and the range will be sufficient for the applications in this book.

THE FIRST PRINCIPLE FOR UNDERSTANDING DATA

Many years ago Dr. Walter Shewhart gave two rules for the presentation of data. They are the basis for honest statistics and should be used as a guide in every presentation of data. His two rules are paraphrased and discussed below.

Shewhart's Rule One for the Presentation of Data:

Data should always be presented in such a way
that preserves the evidence in the data
for all the predictions that might be made from these data.

This rule suggests several things. First of all, a table of the values should accompany most graphs. Second, a table of values is not sufficient to convey the big picture. We are visually oriented, and tables of data are visually boring. A graph (such as a time series graph or a histogram) should accompany any table. Third, the context for the data should be completely and fully described. This would include the answers to: Who collected the data? How were the data collected? When were the data collected? Where were the data collected? What do these values represent? And if the data are computed values, how were the values computed from the raw inputs? Has there been a change in the formula over time?

If a graph is worth a thousand words, then an annotated graph with this supporting information is easily worth ten thousand words. While short summaries of a set of values may be required, they should always be backed up with annotated graphs. Data cannot be divorced from their context without the danger of distortion.

Shewhart's Rule Two for the Presentation of Data:

Whenever an average, range, or histogram is used to summarize data,
the summary should not mislead the user into taking any action
that the user would not take if the data were presented in a time series.

Averages, ranges, and histograms all obscure the time-order for the data. If the time-order for the data shows some sort of definite pattern, then the obscuring of this pattern by the use of averages, ranges, or histograms can mislead the user. Since all data occur in time, virtually all data will have a time-order. In some cases this time-order is the essential context which must be preserved in the presentation.

These rules of Dr. Shewhart's can be summarized in one overriding principle which is the first principle for understanding data and communicating with data.

THE FIRST PRINCIPLE FOR UNDERSTANDING DATA

> *No data have meaning*
> *apart from their context.*

Three consequences of this first principle are:

- Trust no one who cannot, or will not,
  provide the context for their figures.

- Stop reporting comparisons between pairs of values
  except as part of a broader comparison.

- Start using graphs to present current values in context.

SUMMARY

- No comparison between two values can be global.

- Management reports are full of limited comparisons.

- Graphs make data more accessible to the human mind than do tables.

- Numerical summaries of data may supplement graphs, but they can never replace them.

- No data have meaning apart from their context.

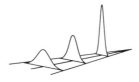

TWO

KNOWLEDGE IS ORDERLY AND CUMULATIVE

Many years ago, David Chambers found the following time series on the wall of the office of the president of a shoe company. Here was a simple and powerful presentation of data in context. The caption on the vertical axis was "Daily Percentage of Defective Pairs."

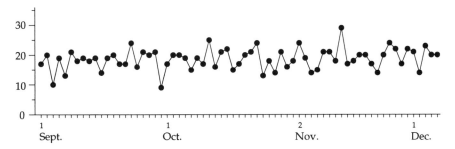

Figure 2.1: Daily Percentage of Defective Pairs

Intrigued, David asked the president why he had the graph on the wall. The president condescendingly replied that he had the chart on the wall so he could tell how the plant was doing.

David immediately responded with, "Tell me how you're doing."

Evidently no one had had the temerity to ask the president this, because he paused, looked at the chart on the wall, and then said, "Well, some days are better than others!"

Input   *Transformation*   *Output*

Figure 2.2: Making Sense of Data Is a Process

Even though the president had his data displayed in a suitable graphic format, and even though he felt that these data were important enough to require their posting each day, *he did not have a way to analyze these values and interpret them.* Or at least he did not have a formal way of analyzing them—he just used a seat-of-the-pants analysis.

No matter what the data, and no matter how the values are arranged and presented, you must always use some method of analysis to come up with an interpretation of the data.

Data have to be filtered in some manner to make them intelligible. This filtration may be based upon a person's experience plus his presuppositions and assumptions, or it may be more formalized and less subjective, but there will always be some method of analysis. If experience is the basis for interpreting the data, then the interpretation is only as good as the manager's past experience. If the current situation is outside the manager's experience, then his interpretation of the data may well be incorrect. Likewise, flawed assumptions or flawed presuppositions can also result in flawed interpretations. However, in the absence of a formal and standardized approach to interpreting data, most managers use the seat-of-the-pants approach and, in the end, about all they can say is that some days appear to be better than others.

The focus of this chapter will be upon the various ways people analyze data. First, two of the more common methods of interpreting data—comparisons to specifications, and comparisons to averages—will be outlined. Next, the process behavior chart approach to the analysis and interpretation of data will be presented and contrasted with the common approaches. Finally, the fundamental difference between the common approaches and the process behavior chart approach will be highlighted by the second principle for understanding data.

COMPARISONS TO SPECIFICATIONS

Plans, goals, budgets, and targets are all specifications. The idea of comparing management data to plans, goals, or budgets was transferred directly from the manufacturing practice of comparing product measurements with specification limits. This type of comparison defines the position of the current value relative to some value (possibly arbitrary), with the outcome being a judgment that the current value is either acceptable or unacceptable (either in-spec or out-of-spec). The fact that this approach to the analysis of data will always result in a favorable or an unfavorable outcome will inevitably lead to a binary world view. Those with favorable figures get a pat on the back, and those with unfavorable figures get kicked a little lower down. Those with favorable figures are "doing okay," while the others are "in trouble."

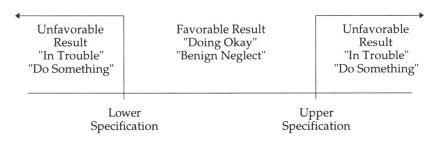

Figure 2.3: The Binary World View of the Specification Approach

A natural consequence of this specification approach to the interpretation of management data is the suddenness with which you can change from a state of bliss to a state of torment. As long as you are "doing okay" there is no reason to worry, so sit back, relax, and let things take care of themselves. However, whenever you are in trouble, "don't just stand there—do something!" Thus, the specification approach to the interpretation of data will inevitably result in periods of benign neglect alternating with periods of intense panic. This on-again, off-again approach is completely antithetical to continual improvement.

The specification approach has both good uses and bad uses. In order to distinguish between these, it is useful to think of specifications for management data as falling into three different categories.[2]

First there are specifications which are facts of life—does the bottom line show a profit or a loss? Are sales growing as fast as the expenses? These are fairly easy to understand. Of course, a specification qualifies as a "fact of life" only if it is known to be true—which is rather different from it being somebody's opinion.

Next there are the specifications needed for planning. Predictions and budgets would typically fall in this category. Such figures should never be arbitrary. Figures needed for planning should always be based upon a careful analysis of the past data plus the present actions plus the likely future conditions. Moreover, predictions and budgets should not be taken as targets. The uncertainties of extending the data from the past into the future makes these values unsuitable as targets. Predictions need knowledge, and they should be used for guidance and help, not for judgment and blame.

Finally, there are specifications which are arbitrary numerical targets. These are totally different from the specifications in the first two categories. While the values in the first two categories are often helpful or even necessary, arbitrary numerical targets are neither helpful nor necessary. In fact they are often detrimental.

---

[2] This distinction was made by Henry Neave in *The Deming Dimension.*

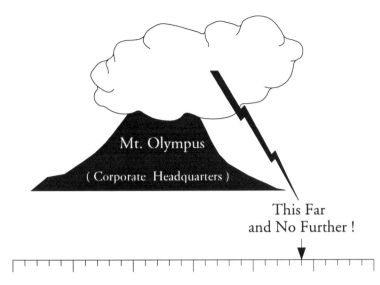

Figure 2.4: The Origin of Many Specifications

Specifications are the *Voice of the Customer.*[3] When the specification is a fact of life, or a figure needed for planning, it is useful to know how the current values compare to the specifications. When the specification is an arbitrary numerical goal, then it can be very dangerous to compare it against the current value. For example, consider an arbitrary production target. If this month's value is above the target, the foreman may be tempted to stockpile the excess and use it against next month's quota. If this month's value is low, then he may be tempted to ship marginal or incomplete items in order to make up the deficit.

In one plant,[4] whenever it became clear that they would not meet the current month's production quota, the foreman would send a forklift to the warehouse to bring back skids of finished product. These units would then be unpacked, loaded on the conveyor, and sent down the

---

[3] Bill Scherkenbach first made this important distinction about the role of specifications relative to a process.

[4] This story is told by Brian Joiner as happening to one of his clients. It beautifully illustrates the problems of arbitrary numerical targets.

packing line. As these units passed down the line, the automatic counters would count them as finished units. As a result of this exercise the department would have another "good" month and the foreman would not have to "explain a bad value." Of course, at the end of the year, the warehouse inventory was short by about a million dollars worth of finished product. This shortage got the plant manager fired. Naturally the new plant manager was nervous. He monitored the routine plant data very carefully, seeking explanations for all values which were unfavorable relative to the targets. Since the pressure to perform was maintained, the production foreman continued as before, and at the end of the fiscal year the warehouse was again about a million dollars short on inventory. The second plant manager was fired.

The new plant manager was *very* nervous. He took inventory after only three months. Of course the warehouse was about a quarter of a million short. At this point the manager took action—he built a fence around the plant site and placed guards at the gates. After another three months he had another inventory done—now they were a half-million short for the year! In desperation the manager built a fence around the warehouse itself and placed a guard on the gate. While this finally stopped the shrinkage in the warehouse, the production figures took a considerable dive.

Notice how the emphasis upon meeting the production target was the origin of all of the turmoil in this case. People were fired and hired, money was spent, all because the production foreman did not like to have to explain, month after month, why they had not met the production quota. When people are pressured to meet a target value there are three ways they can proceed:[5]

1. They can work to improve the system.
2. They can distort the system.
3. Or they can distort the data.

---

[5] Brian Joiner came up with this list several years ago.

Before you can improve any system you must listen to the voice of the system (the *Voice of the Process*). Then you must understand how the inputs affect the outputs of the system. Finally, you must be able to change the inputs (and possibly the system) in order to achieve the desired results. This will require sustained effort, constancy of purpose, and an environment where continual improvement is the operating philosophy.

Comparing numbers to specifications will not lead to the improvement of the process. Specifications are the Voice of the Customer, not the Voice of the Process. The specification approach does not reveal any insights into how the process works.

So if you only compare the data to the specifications, then you will be unable to improve the system, and will therefore be left with only the last two ways of meeting your goal. When a current value is compared to an arbitrary numerical target, the binary world view, which is a consequence of the specification approach, will always create a temptation to make the data look favorable. And distortion is always easier than working to improve the system.

Therefore, while the specification approach will tell you where you are, it will not tell you how you got there, and it will not tell you how to get out of the mess in which you find yourself. While the specification approach may be useful when the specifications are facts of life, or figures needed for planning, the approach becomes meaningless when the specifications are arbitrary targets or goals.

COMPARISONS TO AVERAGES

There are some figures for which the only possible specification is perfection. We want no accidents. We want no spills. We want no workers injured. In such cases it is impossible to compute a percent difference from target—even computers cannot divide by zero. So in order to have a contextual comparison, you will often find the current values compared to an average value.

When values are compared to an average, it is not uncommon to hear a manager ask for an explanation whenever the current value varies more than, say, five percent from the average. Of course, this is just a sophisticated way of saying that one should expect all of the values to fall at, or very close to, the average. If enough pressure is applied, those responsible for coming up with the "explanations" will take steps to avoid having to do so in the future. They will begin to practice one of the two simple "cover your anatomy" techniques—distort the system or distort the data.

Also like the specification approach, the average value approach has two outcomes. You will find the current value to be either "above average" or "below average." Of course, since the average is generally near the mid-point of a set of data, you should expect to be above average about half the time, and to be below average about half the time. A failure to appreciate this simple fact often leads to headlines familiar to all: *"Half the ——— in the state are below average."* Whether it is the reading scores for students, the readiness of fire departments, or the brakes on dump trucks, half of them are bound to be below average on any given day or week. As a consequence, the average value approach will make people feel good about half the time, and it will make them feel bad about half the time.

So, the average value approach to interpreting data has about the same consequences as the specification approach—it has a binary outcome and it yields some knowledge of where the current value stands relative to a fixed reference point. While the specification approach compares the current value with the Voice of the Customer, the average value approach compares the current value with a value from the process itself. Unfortunately, the average value is only *part* of the Voice of the Process. This is why the average value approach can not fully convey the information contained in the current value.

SHEWHART'S APPROACH TO INTERPRETING DATA

We analyze numbers in order to know when a change has occurred in our processes or systems. We want to know about such changes in a timely manner so that we can respond appropriately. While this sounds rather straightforward, there is a complication—the numbers can change even when our process does not. So, in our analysis of numbers, we need to have a way to distinguish those changes in the numbers that represent changes in our process from those that are essentially noise.

To this end Walter Shewhart made a crucial distinction between two types of variation in the numbers. Some variation is routine, run-of-the-mill, and to be expected even when the process has not changed. Other variation is exceptional, outside the bounds of routine, and therefore to be interpreted as a signal of a process change. And in order to separate variation into these two components he created the control chart (which as I noted in the preface, is now being called a process behavior chart).

The process behavior chart begins with the data plotted in a time series. A central line is added as a visual reference for detecting shifts or trends, and limits are computed from the data. These limits are placed symmetrically on either side of the central line at that distance which will allow them to filter out virtually all of the routine variation.

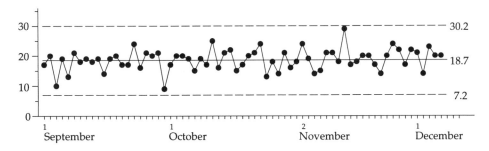

Figure 2.5: Process Behavior Chart for Daily Percentage of Defective Pairs

The key to the effectiveness of the process behavior chart is contained in the way in which the limits are computed from the data. (These calculations will be described in the next chapter.) By characterizing the extent of routine variation, the limits on a process behavior chart allow you to differentiate between routine variation and exceptional variation. If, over a reasonably long period of time, all of the points fall within the limits of a process behavior chart, and if the points are well-behaved, then the process can be said to display nothing but routine variation. When this happens the process can be thought of as being predictable within those limits, and it is reasonable to expect that, unless something is changed, it will continue to operate this way in the future. Thus, the limits on a process behavior chart allow you to characterize the behavior of your process as predictable or unpredictable, and define how much routine variation you should expect in the future. Since prediction is the essence of management, this ability to know what to expect when a process is behaving predictably is invaluable.

However, when points fall outside the limits of a process behavior chart they are interpreted as signs of exceptional variation. Exceptional variation is attributed to assignable causes which, by definition, dominate the many common causes of routine variation. Therefore, when a process displays exceptional variation, it will be worthwhile to seek to identify the assignable cause of that exceptional variation, so that you can eliminate its effect upon your process. In other words, the presence of exceptional variation is a signal that there are dominant cause-and-effect relationships which affect your process and which you are not effectively controlling. Since you would not knowingly allow a dominant cause-and-effect relationship to exist without attempting to control or compensate for it in some manner, it is reasonable to say that exceptional variation is an indication of assignable causes that have escaped your attention. Thus, by separating routine variation from exceptional variation, the process behavior chart allows you to learn about dominant cause-and-effect relationships that may have been overlooked in the past. As you take action to eliminate the effects of assignable causes from your process you will

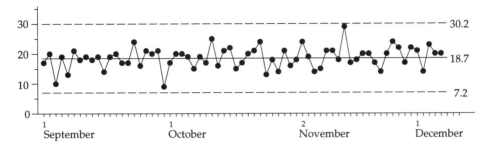

Figure 2.6: Process Behavior Chart for Daily Percentage of Defective Pairs

find that your process will operate more consistently, more predictably, and more reliably. Therefore the process behavior chart can be used to obtain the essential information needed to improve your process when it is subject to exceptional variation.

The process behavior chart in Figure 2.6 shows a time series which consists of 67 consecutive points. The fact that the values remain within the computed limits, and the fact that there is no obvious trend, nor any long sequences of points above or below the central line, suggests that this process may be considered to be predictable. Based on this chart, it would appear that *unless the process is changed in some fundamental way* the plant will continue to produce anywhere from 7% defective to 30% defective each day, with a long-term average of about 19% defective.

Notice how the process behavior chart has helped to interpret the data. First the chart is used to characterize the behavior of the data—are they predictable or not? Second, the process behavior chart allows the manager to predict what to expect in the future—the amount of routine variation defined by the limits is the Voice of the Process.

Finally, notice the difference between the president's interpretation of these data and the interpretation based on the process behavior chart. Some days *only appeared* to be better than others! Thirty-seven days were "worse than average" (i.e. above 18.7%), and 30 days were "better than average," but *the process shows no evidence of any changes during the past 67 days!* In truth, both the "good" days and the "bad" days came from the same process. Unless, and until, this underlying process is changed in some fundamental manner, the president will continue to plot values which average about 19% defective. Looking for differences between the "good" days and the "bad" days will simply be a waste of time.

UNDERSTANDING THE TRADE DEFICITS

The U.S. Trade Deficits for the first ten months of 1987 are given in Figure 2.7. In this period the deficit got worse (increased) relative to the preceding month six times, and it improved (decreased) only three times. While the year started with a deficit of 10.7 billion dollars, by October this had worsened to a deficit of 16 billion dollars. Surely this is justification for gloom and doom.

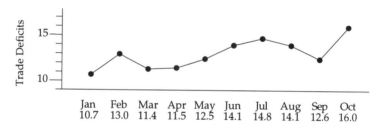

	Jan	Feb	Mar	Apr	May	Jun	Jul	Aug	Sep	Oct
	10.7	13.0	11.4	11.5	12.5	14.1	14.8	14.1	12.6	16.0

Figure 2.7: Time Series Graph for U.S. Trade Deficits, 1987

As each of these values was reported they would invariably be accompanied by statements like "the U.S. trade balance deficit increased (or decreased) last month to a value of — billion dollars." According to the news, the trade balance is always increasing or decreasing. It hardly ever stays the same. But how much of this churning around is signal, and how much of it is just noise?

We begin by placing the data for 1987 on a process behavior chart. The use of one year's worth of data is essentially arbitrary, but we have historically used the calendar to arbitrarily subdivide all sorts of time

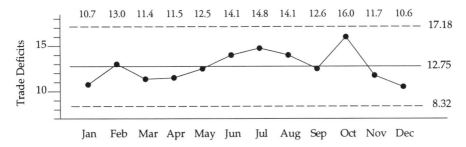

Figure 2.8: Process Behavior Chart for Monthly U.S. Trade Deficits in 1987

series, and we shall, no doubt, continue to do so in the future. While it may be habitual, there is nothing magic about the use of a year's worth of data. The average deficit for 1987 was 12.75 billion dollars. Using the technique which is described in the next chapter, it can be seen that, based on the amount of month-to-month variation, the deficit could vary from 8.32 billion to 17.18 billion without representing a real departure from the average of 12.75 billion.

The chart in Figure 2.8 shows no evidence of a sustained trend. The deficits are not systematically getting better, nor are they systematically getting worse. For the year as a whole, this chart shows no clear-cut evidence of change. Some months *appear* to be better than others, but this chart indicates that it will be a waste to analyze any one month to see what is different from preceding months. You should treat *all* the months of 1987 as if they came from the same system.

The data for 1988 are shown in Figure 2.9. These values could be plotted against the limits shown in Figure 2.8 above. This is done in Figures 2.10 and 2.11.

	Jan	Feb	Mar	Apr	May	Jun	Jul	Aug	Sep	Oct	Nov	Dec
1988	10.0	11.4	7.9	9.5	8.0	11.8	10.5	11.2	9.2	10.1	10.4	10.5

Figure 2.9: Monthly U.S. Trade Deficits, 1988 ($ billions)

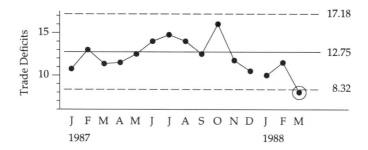

Figure 2.10: Process Behavior Chart for U.S. Trade Deficits, 1987-early 1988

Figure 2.10 shows that by March of 1988 there was definite evidence of an improvement. The March deficit is below the lower limit of 8.32.

Before a single month can be said to signal a change in the time series that single value must go beyond one of the two limits. This happens in March of 1988. Now that we have definite evidence of a change, how do we interpret the chart? One method is to look at the sequence of points adjacent to the point outside the limit which are also on the same side of the central line as the point outside the limit. This sequence is shown in Figure 2.11.

The interpretation of this sequence could be expressed as follows. A change is clearly indicated in March of 1988—it may have begun as early as November of 1987—and it continued throughout the rest of 1988. Thus, there is definite evidence that the trade deficit improved during

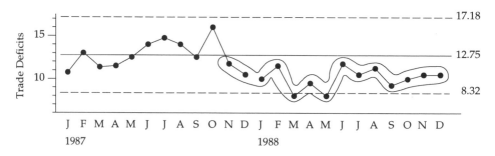

Figure 2.11: Process Behavior Chart for U.S. Trade Deficits, 1987-1988

1988, compared with 1987. We could now recompute limits for 1988 and use them to evaluate further monthly values for signs of improvement or deterioration.

THE SECOND PRINCIPLE
FOR UNDERSTANDING DATA

The process behavior chart approach to the analysis of data is more powerful than either the specification approach or the average value approach. It also is fundamentally different. Instead of attempting to attach a meaning to each and every specific value of the time series, the process behavior chart concentrates on the behavior of the underlying process. It is, therefore, more fundamental and more comprehensive. This is why the process behavior chart yields more insight and greater understanding than the specification approach or the average value approach.

The process behavior chart uses the time series to define the Voice of the Process. It also gives the user a way to know whether it is safe to extrapolate into the near future. Moreover, whenever it is reasonable to make this extrapolation, the process behavior chart also defines the range of values that you are likely to see in the near future. The specification approach and the average value approach do none of these things.

The process behavior chart does all of these things because it takes variation into account. *Variation is the random and miscellaneous component that undermines the simple and limited comparisons.* The "noise" introduced by routine variation is what confuses and clouds all comparisons between single values. Until you can allow for the noise in a time series, you cannot fully understand just what may be indicated by a single value. Is the current value a "signal" that something has changed, or does the current value differ from the historic average by nothing but "noise"?

The answer to this question is the essence of making sense of any value from a time series.

Of course, before you can ever hope to answer this question, you will have to have some historic values. Next you will have to use these historic values to determine just what the effects of "noise" might be for this particular time series. Then, and only then, can you begin to differentiate between the noise of routine variation and the signals of exceptional variation. This whole process may be summarized in the second principle of understanding and communicating with data.

THE SECOND PRINCIPLE FOR UNDERSTANDING DATA

> *While every data set contains noise,*
> *some data sets may contain signals.*
> *Therefore, before you can detect a signal*
> *within any given data set,*
> *you must first filter out the noise.*

The process behavior chart filters out the noise of routine variation by the construction of the limits. Signals of exceptional variation are indicated by points which fall outside the limits or by obvious non-random patterns of variation around the central line.

This distinction between signals and noise is the foundation for every meaningful analysis of data. It also defines the two mistakes which you can make when you analyze data.

The first mistake is that of interpreting routine variation as a meaningful departure from the past—*interpreting noise as if it were a signal.* Since this mistake will lead to actions which are, at best, inappropriate, and at worst, completely contrary to the proper course of action, this mistake is a source of waste and loss every day.

The second mistake consists of not recognizing when a change has occurred in a process—*failing to detect a signal when it is present.* This mistake is most often found in conjunction with the specification approach to analysis. The underlying process changes, but the values are still within the specification limits, so no one notices.

Clearly, you may avoid the first mistake by never reacting to any value as if it were a signal, but this will guarantee many mistakes of the second kind. Likewise, you may avoid the second type of mistake by reacting to every point as if it were a signal, but this guarantees many mistakes of the first kind.

Those who do not make the distinction between signals and noise will inevitably be biased in one direction or the other. So they will make more mistakes of one type or the other. The process behavior chart strikes a balance between these two errors. The use of the limits to filter out the noise of routine variation will minimize the occurrences of both types of errors.

This is why those who do not use process behavior charts to analyze data will always be at a disadvantage compared to those who do. Unless, and until, you make the distinction between signals and noise, you will remain unable to properly analyze and interpret data. The Second Principle of Understanding Data shows why every effective data analysis begins by separating the potential signals from the probable noise. And process behavior charts are the simplest method that has ever been invented to separate potential signals from probable noise.

Before you can use data to justify any action, you must be able to detect a potential signal within the data. Otherwise you are likely to be interpreting noise. Nobody tunes in and listens to static on a car radio—so why should you try to run your business by listening to, and attempting to interpret, static?

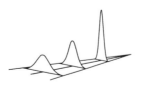

SUMMARY

- The interpretation of data requires a method of analysis.
- Variation is the random and miscellaneous component that undermines the simple and limited comparisons.
- The specification approach always results in a binary world view— you are always either "operating okay" or else "in trouble."
- Specifications which are arbitrary numerical targets are detrimental and counterproductive.
- There are three ways to meet a goal:
    1. Improve the system.
    2. Distort the system, or
    3. Distort the data.
- It is important to distinguish between the Voice of the Customer and the Voice of the Process.
- The specification approach does not consider the Voice of the Process.
- The specification approach and the average value approach attempt to attach a meaning upon each and every value.
- The process behavior chart concentrates upon the behavior of the underlying process.
- A process behavior chart defines the Voice of the Process.
- Prediction requires knowledge—explanation does not.
- A predictable process displays routine variation.
- An unpredictable process displays both routine variation and exceptional variation.
- The first mistake in interpreting data is to interpret noise as if it were a signal.
- The second mistake in interpreting data is to fail to detect a signal when it is present.
- Process behavior charts strike a balance between these two mistakes.

THREE

THE PURPOSE OF ANALYSIS
IS INSIGHT

Data are generally collected as a basis for action. However, unless potential signals are separated from probable noise, the actions taken may be totally inconsistent with the data. Thus, the proper use of data requires that you have simple and effective methods of analysis which will properly separate potential signals from probable noise.

The following examples are intended to illustrate how you can use process behavior charts to gain insight into data. For purposes of comparison, the traditional approaches to management data will be shown alongside the process behavior chart. Each of the situations described below actually happened. Since these stories involve real people in real companies, it was necessary to disguise the data in order to preserve confidentiality. In every other respect these examples are true to the original.

Let us return to the monthly report for July which was first shown in Figure 1.1, and is reproduced in Figure 3.1. When faced with a table of numbers such as that in Figure 3.1 most people begin to scan the percent difference columns to see which numbers have changed the most. The idea is to single out those values which have changed most dramatically and question why they have changed.

Monthly Report for July

Quality:	Dept	July Actual Value	Monthly Average Value	% Diff	% Diff from July Last Year	Year-to-Date Values Actual Value	Plan or Average	% Diff	This YTD as % Diff. of Last YTD
On-Time Shipments (%)	20	91.0	91.3	− 0.3	− 0.9	90.8	91.3	− 0.6	− 0.3
First Time Approval (%)	12	54	70	− 23.0	− 10.0	69.3	70	− 1.0	− 0.4
Pounds Scrapped	19	124	129	− 3.9	0.0	132	129	+ 2.3	+ 1.5
(per 1000 lbs production)									

Production:	Dept	July Actual Value	Monthly Plan Value	% Diff	% Diff from July Last Year	Year-to-Date Values Total or Average	Plan	% Diff	This YTD as % Diff. of Last YTD
Production Volume (1000's lbs)	13	34.5	36.	− 4.2	− 2.0	251.5	252	− 0.2	− 8.0
Material Costs ($/100 lbs)	13	198.29	201.22	− 1.5	− 1.9	198.46	201.22	− 1.4	− 3.6
Manhours per 100 lbs	13	4.45	4.16	+ 7.0	+ 4.5	4.46	4.16	+ 7.2	+ 9.3
Energy & Fixed Costs / 100 lbs	13	11.34	11.27	+ 0.6	+ 11.3	11.02	11.27	− 2.2	+ 9.2
Total Production Costs/100 lbs	13	280.83	278.82	+ 0.7	+ 0.9	280.82	278.82	+ 0.7	+ 0.4
In-Process Inventory (100's lbs)	17	28	19.7	+ 42.0	+ 12.0	21.6	19.7	+ 9.6	+ 5.9

Operations:	Dept	July Actual Value	Monthly Plan Value	% Diff	% Diff from July Last Year	Year-to-Date Values Total or Average	Plan	% Diff	This YTD as % Diff. of Last YTD
On-Time Closings of Accounts (%)	06	74.3	95	− 21.8	− 23.5	87.8	95	− 7.6	− 2.7

Figure 3.1: A Typical Management Report

Of course there are three problems with the use of percent differences as a basis for interpreting the values in a monthly report.

First, the size of the percent difference will partially depend upon the magnitude of the base number—a ten unit change from 100 to 110 is a 10% change, yet a ten unit change from 300 to 310 is a 3.3% change. Percentages show the *relative* size of a change rather than the actual amount of change. Therefore, comparing one percentage change with another is not a reliable way to find the interesting parts of the data because it does not take into account the difference in the base numbers.

Second, the practice of comparing lines in a monthly report by comparing the size of the percent differences *assumes* that all lines should show the same amount of relative variation month to month. Yet, in any collection of time series, each time series will have its own inherent amount of month-to-month variation. Some lines will show large percent differences month to month, and others will show small percent differences from month to month. Therefore, comparing percent differences will guarantee that some lines receive more attention than they deserve while others receive less attention than they deserve.

Third, when considering the percent differences based upon a comparison of the current value with last year's value, a large percent difference may be due to an *unusual value in the past* rather than an *unusual value in the present.*

All of these problems make the comparison of percent differences a weak and unreliable guide to finding the potential signals within the data. Nevertheless, it is a common practice, so we shall use it to select certain lines out of the monthly report for discussion.

As we scan the percent difference column under the July portion of the monthly report three lines stand out. First-time approvals are down 23 percent, in-process inventory is up 42 percent, and on-time closings of accounts is down 21.8 percent.

PROCESS BEHAVIOR CHARTS
FOR INDIVIDUAL VALUES AND MOVING RANGES

Since the monthly meeting would probably focus on the 42 percent increase in the in-process inventory value for Department 17, we will also begin with this line from the monthly report. First we will consider the usual approach to interpreting management data, and then we will use these values to illustrate the construction of a process behavior chart.

Production:	Dept	July Actual Value	Monthly Plan Value	% Diff	% Diff from July Last Yr	Year-to-Date Values Total or Average	Plan	% Diff	This YTD as % Diff. of Last YTD
In-Process Inventory (100's lbs)	17	28	19.7	+ 42.0	+ 12.0	21.6	19.7	+ 9.6	+ 5.9

Monthly Report for July

Figure 3.2: In-Process Inventory for Dept. 17

In July the in-process inventory value was 28. This was the largest value for in-process inventory ever recorded in Department 17. This value was 12% above the value for last July, which is bad, and it was 42% above the plan value, which is very bad. For this year as a whole, the year-to-date in-process inventory is running 5.9% above last year and 9.6% above plan—two more bad values.

If you had responsibility for Department 17 and were shown these data, what would you do? When you have four bad numbers in a row you usually get to prepare a report.

The main problem with the "write a report" approach is the *creativity* required in its preparation. These reports often become works of fiction whose only purpose is to allow a manager to pretend that something is being done about a perceived problem.

In this case the "write a report" approach has a problem with the data themselves. In-process inventory is a *result*, not a *cause*, and it cannot be directly managed. It can only be changed by actions which affect the causes. However, many of these causes will also affect other outputs and parts of the process. So, if you are not careful, pressure to reduce the in-process inventory may have a detrimental effect on some other characteristic of the process such as production volumes. (Remember the three ways of meeting a goal?)

Of course the whole "write a report" approach is based upon the assumption that the in-process inventory value for July is a signal. But is it a signal—or is it just noise? How can you know?

	Jan	Feb	Mar	Apr	May	Jun	Jul	Aug	Sep	Oct	Nov	Dec
In-process Inventory for Department 17 (Hundreds of Pounds)												
Year One	19	27	20	16	18	25	22	24	17	25	15	17
Year Two	20	22	19	16	22	19	25	22	18	20	16	17
Year Three	20	15	27	25	17	19	28					

Figure 3.3: In-Process Inventory Values

Before you can detect a potential signal within the data you must first filter out the probable noise. And to filter out noise you must start with the past data. The table in Figure 3.3 shows the in-process inventory values for Department 17 for the past 31 months.

The average of the 24 values for Years One and Two is 20.04. This value was used as the central line in the time-series graph of the in-process inventory values seen in Figure 3.4.

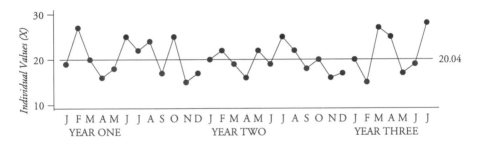

Figure 3.4: Time Series for Monthly In-Process Inventory

A glance at Figure 3.4 shows no long-term trends, nor any other systematic patterns.[6] So while the time series graph adds to our understanding of the data as a whole, it still does not answer the question of whether or not the July value is exceptional. To answer this question we will have to filter out the routine month-to-month variation, which means that we shall have to *measure* the month-to-month variation.

---

6   The gaps in the running record are visual breaks used to delineate the data for each year. They have no other meaning in this, or in subsequent, graphs.

FINDING THE MOVING RANGES

To measure the month-to-month variation we compute the differences between the successive monthly values. These values are called *moving ranges*. They are computed in the following manner.

	Moving Ranges for the In-process Inventory Values (Year One) (differences of successive values)											
	Jan	Feb	Mar	Apr	May	Jun	Jul	Aug	Sep	Oct	Nov	Dec
Year One	19	27	20	16	18	25	22	24	17	25	15	17
mR Values		*8*	*7*	*4*	*2*	*7*	*3*	*2*	*7*	*8*	*10*	*2*

Figure 3.5: Moving Ranges for In-Process Inventory for Year One

The difference between the January value of 19 and the February value of 27 is 8, thus the first moving range is 8.

The next moving range is 7. It is the difference between the February value of 27 and the March value of 20.

The third moving range is 4. It is the difference between the March value of 20 and the April value of 16.

Continuing in this manner, using all 31 values from Figure 3.3, we obtain the 30 moving ranges shown in Figure 3.6.

	Moving Ranges for In-process Inventory for Department 17											
	Jan	Feb	Mar	Apr	May	Jun	Jul	Aug	Sep	Oct	Nov	Dec
Year One		8	7	4	2	7	3	2	7	8	10	2
Year Two	3	2	3	3	6	3	6	3	4	2	4	1
Year Three	3	5	12	2	8	2	9					

Figure 3.6: Moving Ranges for In-Process Inventory

The time series graph of these moving ranges is shown in Figure 3.7. These moving ranges directly measure the month-to-month variation. Their average will be called the *Average Moving Range*. The central line for the time series graph of the moving ranges is commonly taken to be the Average Moving Range.

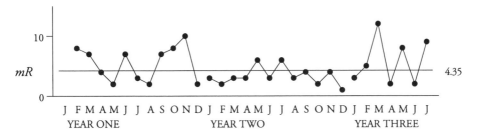

Figure 3.7: Graph of the Moving Ranges

THE TWO GRAPHS IN AN *XMR* CHART

To construct a process behavior chart for *Individual Values and a Moving Range* (an *XmR chart)* we begin with the two time series graphs shown in Figures 3.4 and 3.7. First these two graphs are shown together, as in Figure 3.8.

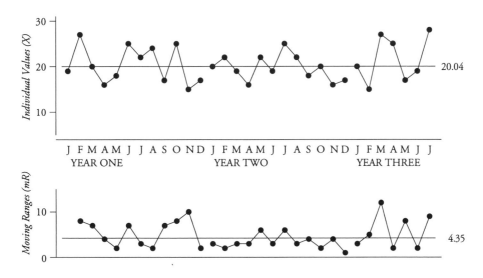

Figure 3.8: Combined Time Series Graphs

The time series for individual values is sometimes referred to as *"the X-chart."* The time series for the moving ranges is sometimes referred to as *"the range chart,"* or *"the moving range chart."* Once the time series graphs for the individual values and the moving ranges have been constructed, the central lines for each graph are computed. The average of the individual values is the usual central line for the X-chart. The Average Moving Range is the usual central line for the moving range chart. The average for Years One and Two is 20.04, and the Average Moving Range is 4.35. These lines are shown in Figure 3.8.

COMPUTING LIMITS FOR AN *XMR* CHART

To obtain the *Upper Range Limit* for the moving range chart you must multiply the Average Moving Range by a scaling factor of 3.27. This value of 3.27 is the number required to convert the average range into an appropriate upper bound for ranges. The value of 3.27 is a constant for this type of process behavior chart.

$$\textit{Upper Range Limit} \;=\; \textit{URL} \;=\; 3.27 \times \overline{mR} \;=\; 3.27 \times 4.35 \;=\; 14.2$$

This Upper Range Limit is plotted as a horizontal line on the moving range portion of the combined graph. This line is shown in Figure 3.9.

The limits for the Chart for Individual Values (the X-chart) are commonly called the *Natural Process Limits*. They are centered on the central line. The distance from the central line to either of these limits is computed by multiplying the Average Moving Range by a second scaling factor: 2.66. The value of 2.66 is constant for this type of process behavior chart—it is the value required to convert the Average Moving Range into the appropriate amount of spread for the running record of individual values.

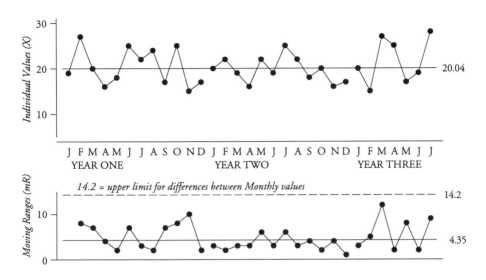

Figure 3.9: Upper Limit for Moving Range Chart

The *Upper Natural Process Limit* is found by first multiplying the Average Moving Range by 2.66 and then adding the product to the central line of the *X*-chart.

$$Upper\ Natural\ Process\ Limit\ =\ \overline{X}\ +\ (\ 2.66\ \times\ \overline{mR}\ )$$
$$=\ 20.04\ +\ (\ 2.66 \times\ 4.35\ )\ =\ 31.6$$

The *Lower Natural Process Limit* is found by first multiplying the Average Moving Range by 2.66 and then subtracting the product from the central line of the *X*-chart.

$$Lower\ Natural\ Process\ Limit\ =\ \overline{X}\ -\ (\ 2.66\ \times\ \overline{mR}\ )$$
$$=\ 20.04\ -\ (\ 2.66 \times 4.35\ )\ =\ 8.5$$

These Natural Process Limits are plotted on the individual values portion of the combined graph. The complete *XmR* chart is shown in Figure 3.10.

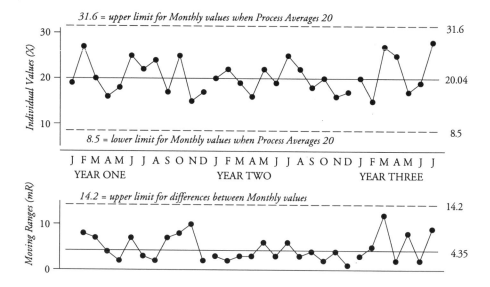

Figure 3.10: XmR Chart for In-Process Inventory

INTERPRETING THE XMR CHART

The interpretation of the process behavior chart in Figure 3.10 is as follows. The month-to-month variation is seen on the moving range portion of the chart. The Upper Range Limit of 14.2 means that if the amount of in-process inventory changes (up or down) by more than 1420 pounds from one month to the next, then you should look for an explanation. A change of this amount from one month to the next is excessive, and it is likely to be the direct result of some assignable cause.

The actual monthly values are seen on the individual values portion of the chart. The limits on this part of the chart define how large or how small a single monthly value must be before it represents a definite departure from the historic average. Here, a monthly value in excess of 31.6

would be a signal that the amount of in-process inventory had shifted upward. Likewise, a monthly value below 8.5 would be taken as a signal of a downward shift. In either case, you would be justified in looking for an assignable cause of such a shift.

Thus, the July value of 28 is not, by itself, a signal. There is no evidence of any real change in the in-process inventory. This means that asking for an explanation for the July value would be an exercise in futility. The man-in-the-moon would be as valid an explanation as any found in a written report.

Now some may feel disconcerted when they see limits for individual values which go from 8.5 to 31.6. Surely we can hold the in-process inventory more steady than that! But that is precisely what cannot be done. At least it cannot be done unless fundamental changes are made in the underlying process. The Natural Process Limits are the Voice of the Process. They define what the process will deliver *as long as it continues to operate as consistently as possible.*

When a process is operated predictably it is also operating as consistently as possible. The process doesn't really care whether or not you like the Natural Process Limits, and it certainly does not know what the specifications may be (specifications should be thought of as the Voice of the Customer, which is distinctly different from the Voice of the Process).

Therefore, if the manager of Department 17 issued a decree that the in-process inventory should not vary by more than ± 20 percent from its average value, what would happen? A ± 20 percent variation from a value of 20.0 is 16.0 to 24.0. Is this process going to operate within these limits? The process behavior chart says that it has not done so in the past, and it should not be expected to do so in the future—at least not without some fundamental change in the underlying process. Thus, such a decree will simply encourage the workers in Department 17 to distort the system or to distort the data. Such decrees, by themselves, do nothing to change or improve the system.

Likewise, dissatisfaction with the Natural Process Limits cannot be cured by finding some alternative method for computing the Natural

Process Limits. Any method that results in appreciably different limits is simply incorrect.[7] The Voice of the Process will still be defined by the limits computed in the manner given above.

Therefore, if you are not pleased with the amount of variation shown by the Natural Process Limits, then you must go to work on the system, to change the underlying process, rather than setting arbitrary goals, jaw-boning the workers, or looking for alternative ways of computing the limits.

---

[7]   A valid alternative for computing limits for the *XmR* chart is to use the Median Moving Range instead of the Average Moving Range. When this is done the scaling factors have to be changed. The value of 2.66 is changed to 3.14, and the value of 3.27 is changed to 3.87.

Using all 31 individual values for the in-process inventory you would get an Average of 20.39, while the 30 moving ranges would have a Median Moving Range of 3.5. With the formulas given on page 136 you would get the limits shown in the following *XmR* chart.

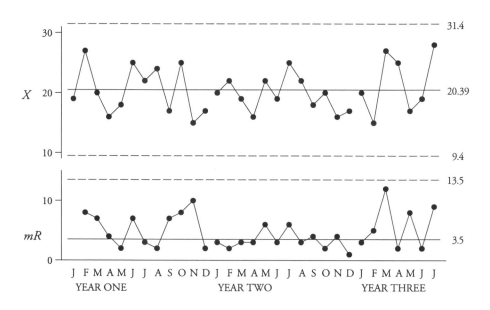

While the limits above are slightly different from those in Figure 3.10 they are not appreciably different, and the story they tell remains the same.

A CHART FOR ON-TIME SHIPMENTS

Now return to the monthly report for July (Figure 3.1) and look for the line with the smallest percent differences. The line for "on-time shipments" is the winner in this category. In most discussions of the monthly report this line would get little more than a cursory glance.

		Monthly Report for July						
Quality:	Dept	July Actual Value	Monthly Average Value	% Diff	% Diff from July Last Yr	Actual Value	Year-to-Date Values Plan or Average	% Diff	This YTD as % Diff. of Last YTD
On-Time Shipments (%)	20	91.0	91.3	– 0.3	– 0.9	90.8	91.3	– 0.6	– 0.3

Figure 3.11: On-Time Shipments for July

In July, 91.0% of the shipments were shipped on time. This is 0.3% below the historic average, and 0.9% below the value for last July. The year-to-date value is 90.8% shipped on time, which is 0.6% below the average and 0.3% below last year. Thus, by these traditional comparisons, the on-time shipments performance is slightly below, but essentially unchanged from last year. Nothing to get excited about here—or is there? How can you know?

We shall put these data on an *XmR* chart.[8] The raw data for the past 31 months are shown in Figure 3.12. The percentage of on-time shipments for each month is computed by dividing the total number of shipments into the total number of shipments which were made on or before the customer request date.

---

8   For those who expected a *p*-chart with these data, see note on page 138.

Percentage On-Time Shipments, Department 20

Month Year	Total No. Shipments	No. Shipped On-Time	Percentage Shipped On-Time	Moving Ranges
January 01	191	176	92.1	—
February 01	203	186	91.6	0.5
March 01	220	202	91.8	0.2
April 01	200	183	91.5	0.3
May 01	236	215	91.1	0.4
June 01	213	194	91.1	0.0
July 01	212	191	90.1	1.0
August 01	241	215	89.2	0.9
September 01	159	143	89.9	0.7
October 01	217	197	90.8	0.9
November 01	181	165	91.2	0.4
December 01	113	103	91.2	0.0
January 02	170	155	91.2	0.0
February 02	270	246	91.1	0.1
March 02	167	151	90.4	0.7
April 02	216	196	90.7	0.3
May 02	227	206	90.7	0.0
June 02	149	136	91.3	0.6
July 02	182	167	91.8	0.5
August 02	224	206	92.0	0.2
September 02	246	225	91.5	0.5
October 02	185	170	91.9	0.4
November 02	261	239	91.6	0.3
December 02	140	128	91.4	0.2
January 03	216	198	91.7	0.3
February 03	247	225	91.1	0.6
March 03	230	209	90.9	0.2
April 03	265	239	90.2	0.7
May 03	184	165	89.7	0.5
June 03	207	188	90.8	1.1
July 03	178	162	91.0	0.2

Figure 3.12: The On-Time Shipments Data

The limits will be based, somewhat arbitrarily, upon the data for Year Two. Columns two and three of Figure 3.12 show that 2225 of the 2437 shipments in Year Two were shipped on time, for an annual percentage of 91.30%. This value will be used as the central line for the individual values. Using the 12 moving ranges for Year Two, the Average Moving Range is computed to be 0.317. This value will be used as the central line for the moving ranges.

Using these values, the Natural Process Limits are computed as:

$$UNPL = 91.30 + (2.66 \times .317) = 92.14\%$$
$$LNPL = 91.30 - (2.66 \times .317) = 90.46\%$$

And the Upper Range Limit for the moving range chart will be:

$$URL = 3.27 \times 0.317 = 1.037\%$$

The *XmR* chart for the on-time shipments is shown in Figure 3.13. It would be interpreted as follows. Allowing for the month-to-month variation, if the shipping process was operating as consistently as possible, with an average of 91.30 percent on-time shipments, then the monthly values should fall between 90.46 percent and 92.14 percent. Moreover, the values for successive months should differ by no more than 1.037 percentage points.

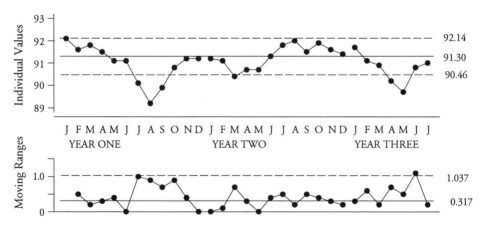

Figure 3.13: *XmR* Chart for On-Time Shipments

Six of the individual values and one of the moving ranges fall outside the limits shown in Figure 3.13. Thus, once the routine month-to-month variation has been taken into account, *there is still too much variation in this time series to be due to chance alone.* The six values below the Natural Process Limit should be treated as signals. You should have looked for an explanation of why the percentage of on-time shipments dropped during these months.

The six values outside the Natural Process Limits are exceptional. The process is trying to tell you that it has a problem. Something was happening in the Summer of Year One, in March of Year Two, and in April and May of Year Three. This something could reoccur, and it could be worse next time.

- You have already missed three opportunities to improve this process.

- The process has already done all that it can do to alert you to the presence of this problem.

- How many more signals are you going to miss before this problem causes you to lose a large account?

- If you concentrate on the percent differences in the monthly report (Figure 3.11) you are not likely to ever be aware of this problem until it is already too late.

Process behavior charts are the way to listen to your process. When you listen to the Voice of the Process as revealed by process behavior charts, you can often detect signals that you would otherwise miss.

THE PREMIUM FREIGHT DATA

A large assembly and manufacturing facility receives thousands of shipments from their suppliers each month. Most of these shipments are shipped by surface freight. Some are shipped by air freight (also known as premium freight). When the general manager asked for a breakdown on the use of surface and air freight the data in Figure 3.14 were assembled by the transportation manager.

Premium Freight Percentages

Month Year	Total No. Shipments	No. Shipped Air Freight	Percentage Shipped Air Freight	Moving Ranges
January 01	5858	619	10.57	—
February 01	4084	451	11.04	0.47
March 01	5196	480	9.24	1.80
April 01	4172	450	10.79	1.55
May 01	6144	374	6.09	4.70
June 01	3792	227	5.99	0.10
July 01	4792	278	5.80	0.19
August 01	7226	346	4.79	1.01
September 01	4440	161	3.63	1.16
October 01	4896	232	4.74	1.11
November 01	6019	352	5.85	1.11
December 01	4101	277	6.75	0.90
January 02	3775	252	6.68	0.07
February 02	5068	229	4.52	2.16
March 02	4119	252	6.12	1.60
April 02	4075	232	5.69	0.43
May 02	4040	239	5.92	0.23
June 02	4038	274	6.79	0.87
July 02	5275	324	6.14	0.65
August 02	4059	268	6.60	0.46
September 02	5133	361	7.03	0.43
October 02	5311	487	9.17	2.14
November 02	2977	290	9.74	0.57
December 02	5658	506	8.94	0.80
January 03	3801	316	8.31	0.63
February 03	4142	359	8.67	0.36
March 03	7585	714	9.41	0.74
April 03	7357	588	7.99	1.42
May 03	3768	445	11.81	3.82
June 03	4050	535	13.21	1.40
July 03	5546	654	11.79	1.42

Figure 3.14: The Premium Freight Data

The transportation manager began by placing the data for the first year on an *XmR* chart.[9] For Year One, 4,247 of the 60,720 shipments were shipped by air. This gives an average of 6.99 percent. The Average

---

9   For those who expected a *p*-chart with these data, see note on page 138.

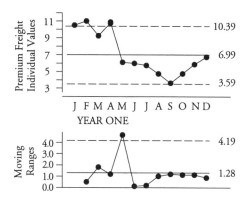

Figure 3.15: *XmR* Chart for Premium Freight

Moving Range for Year One is 1.28 percent. Using these values the *XmR* chart will have the limits shown in Figure 3.15.

Clearly, the percentage of premium freight shipments has changed during this period. The large shift between April and May of the first year results in a moving range which is above the Upper Range Limit. This signifies a break in the time series. When this happens it is appropriate to ask what happened between April and May of the first year.

Upon investigation, the transportation manager found that a series of meetings between manufacturing, purchasing and transportation had been held during April. In these meetings a set of guidelines had been developed for when to use, and when not to use, premium freight. Thus, during April they had changed the system. *The data from the first four months did not come from the same system as the data for the last eight months of Year One.* Based on this information, the manager revised the limits for the chart by deleting the first four values and the first four moving ranges from the computations. The revised *XmR* chart is seen in Figure 3.16.

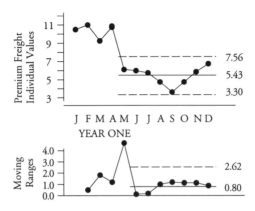

Figure 3.16: Revised *XmR* Chart for Year One

The guidelines for the use of premium freight had the desired effect. Allowing for the month-to-month variation, the percentage of premium freight shipments might go as high as 7.6 percent, or drop to 3.3 percent, but at the end of Year One it was averaging about 5.5 percent, rather than the 10 percent or so seen at the start of the year. Moreover, the percentages of premium freight appear to be predictable. This predictability makes it much easier to budget and plan.

The limits shown in Figure 3.16 were then applied to the remainder of the time series. This *XmR* chart is shown in Figure 3.17. There we can see that the guidelines continued to be effective for the better part of Year Two.

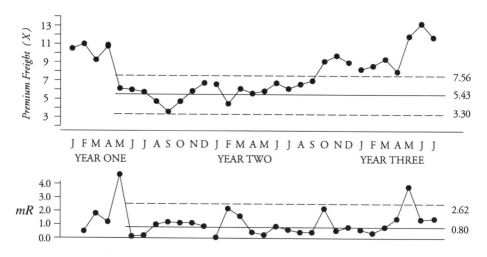

Figure 3.17: *XmR* Chart for Premium Freight Data

However, in the last three months of Year Two, and continuing into Year Three, the percentage of premium freight shipments has definitely increased. Thus, the guidelines worked for about 17 months and then something changed. The chart does not tell us what changed, but it does tell us that a change has occurred and when it happened.

The moving range for May of Year Three is above the limit, which suggests another break in the time series. Subsequent to this large moving range we see three large values on the *X*-chart. Thus, it would appear that, in addition to the change in October of Year Two, there was another change in this system in May of Year Three.

This last increase in the percentage of premium freight drew attention to itself by crossing the boundary from single digit values to double digit values. Transitions of this type are easier to spot in the monthly reports, and thus the general manager asked for the transportation department to look into the use of premium freight. If all of these values were 3.0 units smaller, this transition from single digits to double digits would not have occurred, and the second signal would have probably gone unnoticed as well.

By failing to use process behavior charts to track their time series, the managers in this plant missed seven or eight months worth of signals. They *assumed* that their guidelines were working long after they had ceased to work. As Dr. Deming has noted, this is a good way to *maximize* your costs.

SO WHAT'S THE DIFFERENCE?

In the first example (in-process inventories) the manager assumed that a large percent difference had to represent a signal. Yet an analysis of the data revealed that there was no signal. The high value was well within the Natural Process Limits, and therefore should be considered to be routine. By interpreting routine variation as a signal, the manager caused those who were asked to explain noise to waste both time and effort. Mistakes like this can lead to the distortion of the system or the distortion of the data. Thus, this mistake wasted time, wasted resources, and wasted emotional energy—all of which could have been better used in working to improve the system.

In the second example (on-time shipments) signals were missed by the traditional approach because of the small percent differences shown in the monthly report. *A missed signal is an opportunity wasted.* The process tried to indicate that there was a problem, but no one noticed. When no one notices a problem, it is likely to persist and may even grow bigger. While it remains unnoticed it will still have a detrimental effect upon operations. This will result in increased costs, decreased reliability, and potential loss of business. In the case of the on-time shipments, the problem will have to get much larger before it will be noticed using the traditional techniques. By that time it may be too late to repair the damage done.

In the third example (premium freight) the managers did finally notice something happening—long after the initial change. With the traditional approach they finally found something happening between April and May of Year Three. While the process behavior chart shows that something happened between April and May, it also shows a change around October of Year Two which was missed by the traditional approach.

In any study, success will often depend upon knowing what questions to ask. The process behavior chart is unsurpassed for focusing data so that the user can formulate the interesting and important questions.

So what's the difference between the traditional, limited comparisons and the process behavior chart? *The difference between superstition and knowledge.*

The traditional approach inevitably results in wasted effort and missed opportunities. The use of traditional approaches guarantees an excess of both kinds of mistakes people make when interpreting data. More often than necessary, managers interpret some bit of noise as a signal, and thereby waste time and resources in looking for an explanation that does not exist. On the other hand, many signals, and the opportunity for improvement which these signals represent, are missed by the traditional approach.

The process behavior chart filters out the probable noise in order to detect the potential signals in any data set. By filtering out the noise, the process behavior chart will minimize the number of times that you will interpret a bit of noise as if it were a signal. By causing the potential signals to stand out, the process behavior chart will also minimize the number of times that you will miss a signal. Thus, process behavior charts are the beginning of knowledge because they help you to ask the right questions.

Everybody needs this kind of help.

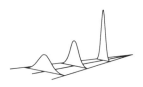

MONTHLY RECEIPTS

Premium payments constitute a major portion of the income for a regional insurance company. The company tracks premium payments on a monthly basis and includes them in their monthly report. The receipts from policies in force for the first six months of Year One, in thousands of dollars, are listed in Figure 3.18.

	Receipts from Policies in Force (Thousands of Dollars)					
	Jan	Feb	Mar	Apr	May	Jun
Year One	13,463	13,468	13,456	13,458	13,465	13,455
Moving Ranges		5	12	2	7	10

Figure 3.18: Monthly Receipts for Insurance Company

The average of these monthly receipts is 13,460.8. The Average Moving Range is 7.2. These values result in the *XmR* chart shown in Figure 3.19.

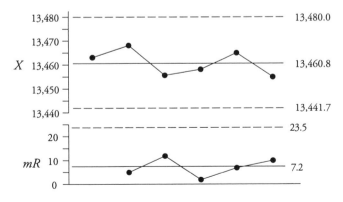

Figure 3.19: First *XmR* Chart for Monthly Receipts

Given the current level of activity, and the amount of month-to-month variation, you could expect the monthly receipts to vary from 13,441.7 to 13,480.0. The month-to-month changes should average about 7.2 thousand, and any month-to-month change which exceeds 23.5 thousand is a signal of a change.

The receipts for the next six months are shown in Figure 3.20. These six values average 13,465.0. Have the monthly receipts increased? While you may be pleased that the values are, in general, larger than before, the real question is whether or not collections have actually increased—or is this just an aberration that has no underlying assignable cause? The easy way to answer this question is to use the process behavior chart. The 12 values for Year One are shown on an *XmR* chart in Figure 3.21. The limits shown came from the *XmR* chart in Figure 3.19.

	Receipts from Policies in Force (Thousands of Dollars)					
	Jul	Aug	Sep	Oct	Nov	Dec
Year One	13,462	13,453	13,461	13,466	13,478	13,470
Moving Ranges	7	9	8	5	12	8

Figure 3.20: Monthly Receipts for Insurance Company

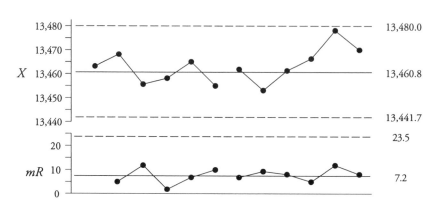

Figure 3.21: Second *XmR* Chart for Monthly Receipts

While the total receipts for the second six months are greater than for the first six months, there is no evidence that this increase is due to any real change in the system that generates these revenues. Two ways that a signal might have made itself known are: a single monthly value beyond a limit or at least three out of four consecutive values which are closer to one of the limits than they are to the central line.[10] Neither of these signs are seen in Figure 3.21.

Since there is no evidence that the second six months are appreciably different from the first six months, you might decide to use all 12 months to revise the computed limits. The average for all 12 months is 13,462.9 and the Average Moving Range is 7.73. The Upper Natural Process Limit is found to be 13,483.5. The Lower Natural Process Limit is found to be 13,442.4. The Upper Range Limit for the moving ranges is found to be 25.3. Thus, the individual monthly collections can vary from 13,442 to 13,463 without signaling a change in the system. These limits are used in Figure 3.23. The collections for the next six months are shown in Figure 3.22.

	Receipts from Policies in Force (Thousands of Dollars)					
	Jan	Feb	Mar	Apr	May	Jun
Year Two	13,459	13,447	13,446	13,439	13,448	13,440
Moving Ranges	11	12	1	7	9	8

Figure 3.22: Monthly Receipts for Insurance Company

These values from Year Two are included with the 12 values from Year One on an *XmR* chart in Figure 3.23.

---

10 Three out of four consecutive values which are closer to one of the limits than they are to the central line may be taken as an indication of a shift even when no single point falls outside that limit. This "run test" is based upon the characteristic that for predictable processes about 85% to 90% of the data will fall *within* the middle one-half of the region defined by the limits (closer to the central line than to either limit). Thus, a sequence of 3 out of 3, or 3 out of 4 such "relatively rare" points (closer to one of the limits than they are to the central line) may be taken to be a signal of exceptional variation.

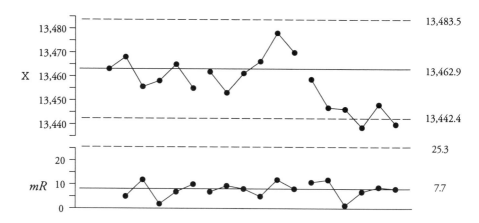

Figure 3.23: Third *XmR* Chart for Monthly Receipts

The values for April and June are below the Lower Natural Process Limit. Even if the April value had not been outside the limits, the values for February, March and May would have signaled a shift. These three values are an example of the 3 out of 4 closer to the limit than to the central line rule.

Thus, there is clear and definite evidence that the collections have dropped, and that this drop is due to some change in the underlying system that generates these revenues. This change is too large to have occurred by chance. It is very likely that there is an assignable cause, and it will be worthwhile to discover just what this assignable cause may be.

Since the system has changed, the last five or six values could be used to compute new limits for use with future values. The data from Year One is no longer characteristic of the process. Continuing this way the value for each month can be plotted as it becomes available. Signals will be detected as soon as they become clear and pronounced, and limits can be revised as appropriate to represent the current status of the system or process. Useful limits may be constructed using as few as five or six consecutive values.

SUMMARY

- Large percent differences do not necessarily indicate a signal.

- Small percent differences do not necessarily indicate a lack of a signal.

- Points outside the limits are signals—they are opportunities to discover how to improve a process. (A large moving range signifies a break in the original time series.) Shewhart argued, and experience has shown, that it is economically worthwhile to investigate all such signals of exceptional variation.

- The process behavior chart focuses data so that the user will ask the interesting and important questions.

- A single value beyond the limits of a process behavior chart is a signal.

- Another pattern which is taken to be a signal consists of at least three out of four consecutive values which are closer to one of the limits than they are to the central line.

- The process behavior chart filters out the probable noise in order to detect the potential signals in any data set.

- By filtering out the noise, the process behavior chart minimizes the number of times that you will interpret a bit of noise as if it were a signal.

- By causing the potential signals to stand out, the process behavior chart will also minimize the number of times that you miss a signal.

- Process behavior charts are the beginning of knowledge because they help you to ask the right questions.

- Formulas for Charts for Individual Values and Moving Ranges are:

Use the individual values to compute the ***Average***, $\overline{X}$.
This value will be the central line for the X-chart.

Find the moving ranges and
compute the ***Average Moving Range***, $\overline{mR}$.
This value will be the central line for the mR chart.

To find the **Upper Natural Process Limit** for the X-chart:
multiply the ***Average Moving Range*** by 2.66
and add the product to the ***Average***.

$$UNPL = \overline{X} + (\, 2.66 \times \overline{mR} \,)$$

To find the **Lower Natural Process Limit** for the X-chart:
multiply the ***Average Moving Range*** by 2.66
and subtract the product from the ***Average***.

$$LNPL = \overline{X} - (\, 2.66 \times \overline{mR} \,)$$

To find the **Upper Range Limit** for the mR chart:
multiply the ***Average Moving Range*** by 3.27.

$$URL = 3.27 \times \overline{mR}$$

- The multiplicative constants of 2.66 and 3.27 seen in the equations above are scaling factors needed to convert the Average Moving Range into the values you need to obtain the appropriate limits for each portion of the XmR chart.

- Useful limits may be constructed with as few as five or six values.

- The uncertainty in the computed limits decreases as the amount of data used to compute the limits increases.

FOUR

THE BEST ANALYSIS
IS THE SIMPLEST ANALYSIS
WHICH GIVES
THE NEEDED INSIGHT

The traditional limited comparisons, in which a current value is expressed as a percentage of some other value, can neither filter out noise nor highlight potential signals. Large percent differences may be due to noise, and small percent differences may represent signals. Managers who use percent differences exclusively will be misled. They will focus on the wrong items and wonder what went wrong as things get worse.

The previous chapters have attempted to outline the need for separating the probable noise from the potential signals. This chapter will continue with examples of how this may be accomplished with management and administrative data.

PREMIUM FREIGHT REVISITED

You should always remember that there are several ways to measure most processes. Consider the Premium Freight Data from the previous chapter—instead of tracking the percentage of shipments, we could have tracked the percentage of shipping costs due to premium freight. These data are given in Figure 4.1.

These financial data are expressed as percentages because the unequal number of shipments each month makes the direct comparison of the costs hard to interpret. By expressing each month's premium freight costs as a percentage of that month's total freight costs, the costs are adjusted for the different levels of activity. This conversion of raw numbers into rates and percentages is often necessary before you can meaningfully compare the month-to-month values. However, it is important to make sure that the adjustments are appropriate for any given time series.

The moving ranges in Figure 4.2 were computed using the percentages shown in Figure 4.1.

					Premium Freight Cost Percentages							
Year	Jan	Feb	Mar	Apr	May	Jun	Jul	Aug	Sep	Oct	Nov	Dec
One	35.9	37.6	34.3	33.6	23.2	22.6	19.1	20.6	23.8	20.7	23.3	19.9
Two	18.2	21.4	21.0	22.4	19.6	19.6	23.4	21.2	22.6	24.7	26.5	31.4
Three	29.1	27.7	30.7	30.2	27.6	29.3	32.2					

Figure 4.1: Percentages of Shipping Costs Due to Premium Freight

				Moving Ranges for Premium Freight Cost Percentages							
Year	Jan	Feb	Mar	Apr	May	Jun	Jul	Aug	Sep	Oct	Nov	Dec
One	–	1.7	3.3	0.7	10.4	0.6	3.5	1.5	3.2	3.1	2.6	3.4
Two	1.7	3.2	0.4	1.4	2.8	0.0	3.8	2.2	1.4	2.1	1.8	4.9
Three	2.3	1.4	3.0	0.5	2.6	1.7	2.9					

Figure 4.2: Moving Ranges for Premium Freight Cost Percentages

Based on the analysis of the percentage of premium freight shipments in the previous chapter, we already know to look for a break between April and May of Year One. The drop in percentages is dramatic, and the moving range of 10.4 in May stands out like a giant. Since the earlier analysis (on page 51) used the data from May to December of Year One to establish the limits for the *XmR* chart, we shall do the same with these data. For these eight months the average of the individual values is 21.65 percent and the average of the seven corresponding moving ranges is 2.56 percent. These values result in the following limits.

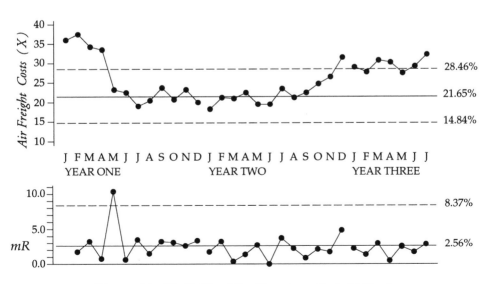

Figure 4.3: *XmR* Chart for Premium Freight Costs

$$\textit{Upper Natural Process Limit} = \overline{X} + (2.66 \times \overline{mR})$$
$$= 21.65 + (2.66 \times 2.56) = 28.46$$

$$\textit{Lower Natural Process Limit} = \overline{X} - (2.66 \times \overline{mR})$$
$$= 21.65 - (2.66 \times 2.56) = 14.84$$

$$\textit{Upper Range Limit} = URL = 3.27 \times \overline{mR} = 3.27 \times 2.56 = 8.37$$

The *XmR* chart for these data is shown in Figures 4.3 and 4.5. This chart reveals the same dramatic and definite difference between April and May of Year One which was seen in Figure 3.17. This change was identified as the result of new guidelines for the use of premium freight. However, there are some differences between the *XmR* chart in Figure 4.3 and that in Figure 3.17 (which is shown below as Figure 4.4). For example, compare the *X*-chart in Figure 4.5 with that in Figure 4.4.

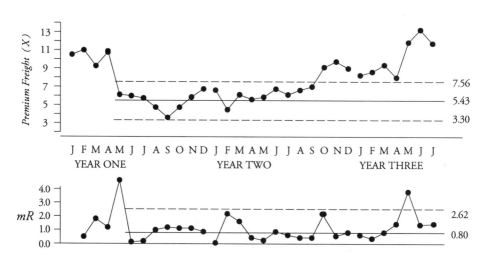

Figure 4.4: *XmR* Chart for Percent Premium Freight Shipments

While both Figures 4.4 and 4.5 indicate that the usage of premium freight has increased in Year Three compared to Year Two, they show the first point outside the limits in different months. The percentage of air shipments signaled a change in October of Year Two, while the percentage of costs for air freight signaled a change in December of Year Two. Thus, these two representations of the premium freight tell the same overall story, but they differ in the details.

The *X*-chart in Figure 4.5 shows that the premium costs became *detectably higher than 21.65 percent* in December of Year Two. However, when we look at the *run*[11] which contains the points outside the limits we see that the run began in September. Thus, while there was a detectable signal in December of Year Two, the problem could have begun as early as September of Year Two.

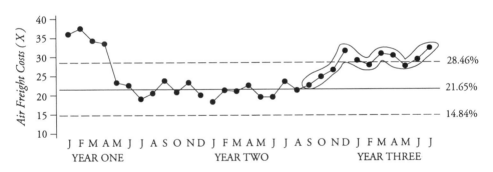

Figure 4.5: Run of Elevated Premium Freight Costs

Thus, both the premium shipment time series and the premium cost time series show a change in the latter part of Year Two. Something happened to change the system at that time. With such strong evidence of a change, you can begin to ask the right questions which will hopefully reveal the assignable cause of this shift. *If you do not use process behavior charts, then it is unlikely that you will detect the shift in a timely manner.*

---

[11]   As used here, a *run* is a sequence of points on the same side of the central line.

Finally, the premium shipment time series in Figure 4.4 shows an additional shift in May of Year Three. The premium cost time series in Figure 4.5 does not show a corresponding increase. Therefore, the change seen in the premium shipment data is likely to be concentrated in the smaller (and cheaper) shipments.

In both Figure 4.4 and Figure 4.3, the Natural Process Limits helped to separate the probable noise from the potential signals. They helped to define when the process actually changed for the worse. Yet, in both graphs *the fact that there had been a change in the recent months was apparent from a simple inspection of the time series graph itself.* The limits just helped to clarify what the graph revealed. The sequence of elevated values during the last eight to ten months was apparent without the limits. This type of signal is also recognized and should be used.

Whenever eight or more successive values fall on the same side of the central line, it is safe to say that the time series has shifted away from the central line. This rule is often used even when none of the individual points fall outside the computed limits. Eight or more successive values on one side of the central line is roughly the same as getting eight or more heads or tails in succession when tossing a coin. The odds for the latter event are commonly cited at less than 1 out of 128. Thus, with odds that are longer than 100 to 1, eight or more successive points on the same side of the central line are most logically interpreted as a signal rather than as noise.

PRODUCTION VOLUMES

One company had a management information system which would allow every manager to access current data for all of the routine measures of plant activity. Now they could all see, on a daily and weekly basis, the levels of activity in each of the various production facilities—no more waiting until the end of the month for big surprises! Of course everyone was proud of this new system, and they were delighted to have the instantaneous feedback.

After the management information system had been in place for a few months one manager decided to plot the weekly production volume for his plant. This plant consisted of a continuous chemical process, run on a 24-hour, seven-day per week basis. The production volumes, reported in thousands of dollars, are shown in Figure 4.6.

					Plant 42						
			Weekly Production Volumes in Thousands of Dollars								
21.6	23.9	23.3	22.6	28.8	22.7	23.8	22.8	28.7	22.9	24.2	23.3
28.6	22.8	23.9	23.2	23.7	28.5	23.2	23.5	23.1	27.7		

Figure 4.6: Plant 42 Weekly Production Volumes

Can you see any problem with the data in Figure 4.6?

Remember, managers traditionally have used the current value to ascertain how they are doing. This table is much more comprehensive than a simple limited comparison. Do you see anything unusual in the data in the table above?

Eyeballing the data in the manner suggested here can be called *analysis by osmosis*—first you are going to soak up the data and then you will understand it.

Analysis by osmosis is not very reliable because it allows different people to detect different things in the same data set. Instead of using analysis by osmosis, it is always much better to graph your data. The time series graph for these weekly production volumes is shown below.

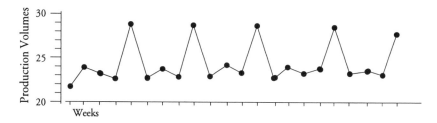

Figure 4.7: Weekly Production Volumes for Plant 42.

How much easier it is to detect patterns with a graph!

The manager knew that this plant was essentially running at capacity. The implied spikes in production simply could not be a characteristic of the physical process. Yet the spikes are a characteristic of the time series. They persist. If they are not part of the production process, then they must be part of the reporting process. *Then* the manager noticed the period of the spikes. Each spike corresponds to the last week in a month.

People were getting behind on their data entry during the month, and getting caught up at the end of each month. So even though the state-of-the-art management information system would give the managers up-to-date data throughout each month, the values were not really up to date.

The moral to this story is: trust no data before its time. In this system the data have to age before they can be used.

This example serves to illustrate the way in which graphic presentations communicate the content of a data set so much more effectively than a table of values. Tables of values tend to overwhelm the user with all kinds of extraneous details. Graphs tend to sweep away the extraneous details and reveal any interesting structures present in the data. This is why the process behavior chart represents such a major advance in understanding data—it is based upon a graph which preserves the time order information.

In some cases, such as this one, the signals are so clear-cut and easy to understand that you will not need to compute limits. The eyeball will naturally filter out the noise. When this happens, the graph is generally sufficient to communicate the results.

FIRST TIME APPROVAL RATES

Returning to the original Monthly Report for July, the First Time Approval Rate for Department 12 showed a current value that was 23% below the average value. Department 12 makes batches of compound. Each batch is tested for conformity to specifications. If every component in the compound is within its specification range on the first test, then the batch is approved on first test. Batches which are not approved on first test are then reworked to bring them into specifications.

The First Time Approval Rate for July is 54%, meaning that 46% of the batches had to be reworked. This is 23% below average and 10% below last July's value. These comparisons make July look like a bad month. However, for the year, the department is right on target with respect to both the average and last year.

Once again, the information provided in the monthly report is only a small piece of the overall picture. The comparisons are limited and hard to interpret. Does a 54% first time approval for July represent an unusual condition or not? How can you know?

		Monthly Report for July						
		July	Monthly		% Diff	Year-to-Date Values		This YTD as
		Actual	Average	%	from July	Actual	Plan or	%	% Diff. of
Quality:	Dept	Value	Value	Diff	Last Yr	Value	Average	Diff	Last YTD
First Time Approval (%)	12	54	70	− 23.0	− 10.0	69.3	70	− 1.0	− 0.4

Figure 4.8: The First Time Approval Rate for July

The First Time Approval Rates for the past 31 months are shown in Figure 4.10. Is there any problem with these data?

	Percentage First Time Approvals for Department 12											
Year	Jan	Feb	Mar	Apr	May	Jun	Jul	Aug	Sep	Oct	Nov	Dec
One	60	57	89	51	53	90	64	69	87	63	55	94
Two	68	60	89	51	68	91	60	54	90	58	65	85
Three	62	66	97	55	56	95	54					

Figure 4.9: First Time Approval Rates for Department 12

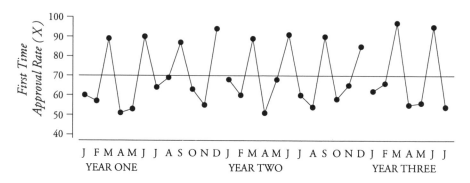

Figure 4.10: Time Series Graph for First Time Approval Rates

What pattern exists in the data shown in Figure 4.10? Would you be surprised to learn that while the monthly First Time Approval Rates are only used in the local plant, the *quarterly rates are reported to corporate headquarters?* What does this piece of information add to the interpretation of the graph in Figure 4.10?

How does Department 12 achieve such outstanding results every third month? And, if they can do it every third month, with such regularity and predictability, why can't they do it every month?

Upon inquiry, it turned out that Department 12 was under an immense amount of pressure to make sure that the quarterly rate was near 70% so that the plant would not receive any "special" attention from corporate headquarters. They dutifully complied by changing the system in the third month of each quarter—they would run a special "preliminary test" on each batch. If the preliminary test showed the batch to be out of specifications, then additional work was done before they would take the "first test" sample. In this way they would boost the First Time Approval Rate for the third month and for the quarter as a whole. Nobody at corporate headquarters asked any questions, so everybody in Department 12 was happy. Isn't it great what creativity in the workplace can do?

The graph shows clearly that there are two different sets of data being mixed together here. The data from the first two months of each quarter averages about 60%. This is a more accurate indicator of what this department is really doing. If the third month from each quarter is dropped from the time series, and the remaining values are placed on an *XmR* chart, the Lower Natural Process Limit for *X* would be about 40%, and the Upper Natural Process Limit would be about 80%. Thus, the July value of 54% is not exceptional, but the values for the third month of each quarter are all clearly and definitely exceptional. As noted earlier, pressure to meet any arbitrary numerical goal or target will most often result in the distortion of either the system, or the data, or both.

THERE IS NOTHING NEW UNDER THE SUN

Surely the nonsense in the preceding section has to be an isolated example—doesn't it? No. Unfortunately it is more the rule than the exception.

A different chemical company from the one described in the preceding section had a monthly management meeting in which the transparency in Figure 4.11 was used. The unit was congratulating themselves for having a perfect month—they had a 100% First Time Approval Rate for the batches produced the previous month. Yet three bullets down the list on the screen they had an item which read "Cost of Scrapping Two Batches: $50,000."

- 100% First Time Approval Rate for Month
- ...
- ...
- Cost of Scrapping Two Batches: $50,000.
- ...

Figure 4.11: Overhead Shown at a Monthly Management Meeting

If all of the batches were good, from where did the scrap batches come? *They came from the preliminary tests.* These two batches were so far out of specification that they could not be reworked. Since they never got to the point of having a "first test" they did not count against the First Time Approval Rate.

Creativity knows no bounds!

POUNDS SCRAPPED

Department 19 produces a sheet product. The edges of this sheet, and the end of each roll, have to be trimmed off as part of the production process. The trimming makes it impossible to get a 100 percent yield from this process. This unavoidable scrap is reported by Department 19 in terms of the number of pounds of scrap per 1000 pounds of finished product. It was shown as a line under the quality section of the monthly report for July.

| | | July | Monthly | | % Diff | Year-to-Date Values | | | This YTD as |
| | | Actual | Average | % | from July | Actual | Plan or | % | % Diff. of |
Quality:	Dept	Value	Value	Diff	Last Yr	Value	Average	Diff	Last YTD
Pounds Scrapped (per 1000 lbs production)	19	124	129	– 3.9	0.0	132	129	+ 2.3	+ 1.5

Monthly Report for July

Figure 4.12: Pounds Scrapped in July

The scrap for July of Year Three was about four percent below average, and it was exactly the same as last July. These values suggest that July was a fairly good month.

For the year, Department 19 is about two percent above average on scrap, and 1.5 percent higher than in July of last year. These values suggest that we may be doing worse this year than last year.

Do these comparisons answer all of your questions about the scrap levels in this process? Are you ready to go on to some other line in the monthly report? For years this is all that managers have had. Surely, it must be enough!

OSHA REPORTABLES

The number of accidents which are reportable under the guidelines and rules of the Occupational Safety and Health Administration are reported each month for the plant as a whole. They are included under the safety section of the monthly report, and are the first topic of discussion in every monthly meeting.

Monthly Report for July									
		July	Monthly		Diff from	Year-to-Date Values			This YTD as
		Actual	Average	%	July			%	% Diff. of
Safety:	Dept	Value	Value	Diff	Last Yr	Total	Average	Diff	Last YTD
OSHA Reportables	All	5	1.5	+ 233	+ 5	13	10.5	+ 24	+ 44

Figure 4.13: OSHA Reportables for July

July, with five accidents, was far above average. This was more than twice as many accidents as usual, and five more than had occurred last July. In fact, this plant had never had five accidents in one month before. For the year, they had had 13 accidents in seven months. This was 24% above average, and 44% ahead of the previous year. All of this bad news seemed to require some sort of action, but what? One executive, when given this report, actually suggested that they should cut the number of OSHA Reportables in half next year!

Think about it—they should aim to have nine accidents next year?

If they can actually cut the accident rate by setting a goal, then why didn't they do it this year?

If they cannot cut the accident rate by setting a goal, then what is the effect of setting a goal?

Accidents are a result, not a cause. They cannot be managed by goal setting. The data may be distorted by pressure to meet goals, but the system that gives rise to accidents will not be affected by any arbitrary numerical target.

Thus, you must *study the system* that gives rise to the accidents, and the only way to do this is to listen to the Voice of the Process—by placing the data on a process behavior chart.

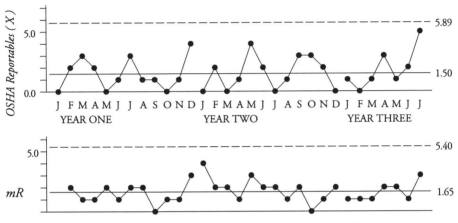

Figure 4.14: *XmR* Chart for OSHA Reportables

Years One and Two show an average of 1.5 OSHA reportables per month. The Average Moving Range for these data is 1.65. Based on these values the Upper Natural Process Limit is 5.9. This means that as long as this plant averages 1.5 accidents per month, there will be occasional months with four or five accidents.

So even though five accidents in a month is undesirable and unacceptable, an occasional month with five accidents is *inevitable* as long as the average is 1.5 accidents per month.

There is no evidence in Figure 4.14 that the system which results in accidents is any different in July than it was in June or May. The accident rate at this plant cannot be said to have improved. Neither can it be said to have gotten worse. The *X*-chart shows a system that is operating in a steady-state mode. As long as the plant averages 1.5 accidents per month, the monthly values will range from zero to five. Before a single month's value can be said to be a signal it will have to be greater than or equal to six.

So how do you go about reducing the number of accidents in this plant? Since the system is stable over time, you can only study the system to see what contributes to accidents. This means that you would study *all* the accidents, in *all* the months. It would be a mistake to single out just the month of July in Year Three. The chart suggests that there are no assignable causes that are inflating the accident rate for any one month. Treat all months alike. Anything else will be based on a misunderstanding of the data and the inability to properly interpret the Voice of the Process.

THE REST OF THE STORY

If you felt satisfied with the treatment of the Pounds Scrapped Data which was given on page 73, then you should skip this section. In fact, you might as well skip the rest of the book—you have a terminal case of numerical naiveté.

For all of you who felt a little bit cheated at the bottom of page 73, here is the rest of the story.

The data for the Pounds Scrapped in Department 19 are given in Figure 4.15. The *XmR* chart for these data is shown in Figure 4.16.

Whether you see it in the table, or spot it on the *X*-chart, there is a definite and persistent pattern to these values. The scrap goes up in the

					Pounds Scrapped per 1000 Pounds Produced							
	Jan	Feb	Mar	Apr	May	Jun	Jul	Aug	Sep	Oct	Nov	Dec
One	133	128	128	123	124	124	126	124	126	124	129	135
Two	142	140	131	126	124	126	124	126	123	125	133	134
Three	134	139	143	131	126	125	124					

Figure 4.15: Pounds Scrapped for Department 19

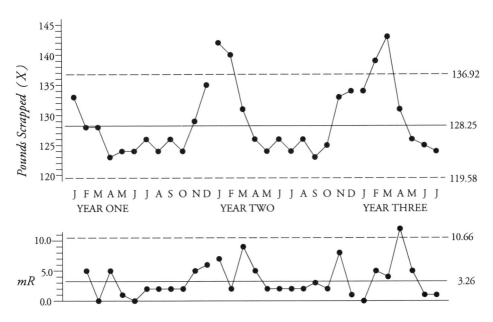

Figure 4.16: ***XmR* Chart for Pounds Scrapped in Department 19**

colder months, and it goes down in the warmer months. Given this pattern, the below average value for July is simply what you should expect. The current year is proceeding as the previous years have done. Thus, in this case, the year-to-date comparisons told the true story, rather than the current value comparisons.

The scrap rate goes up every November, and remains elevated until April of each year. In fact, the large range for April of Year Three suggests that the changeover can be quite rapid. By investigating the points where the changes occur you might be able to remedy this problem.

In another case, where the adhesive strength of a bond was affected by the ambient humidity, the production personnel and the engineers had done everything they could do to fix the seasonal cycle. After six years without success they had pretty well decided that the seasonal cycle was unavoidable. However, when they started using process behavior charts on each step of the production process, and when they were able to operate these process steps predictably, they found that the seasonal cycle disappeared and the overall quality level increased to higher levels than they had ever attained before.[12]

Process behavior charts work. They work when nothing else will work. They have been thoroughly proven. They are not on trial. The question is not whether they will work in your area. The only question is whether or not you will, by using these tools and practicing the way of thinking which goes with them, begin to get the most out of your processes and systems.

The alternative is to be left behind.

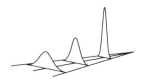

---

[12] The details of this example are given in the last section of Chapter 11 of *Understanding Statistical Process Control, Second Edition.*

SUMMARY

- Traditional limited comparisons can neither filter out the noise nor highlight potential signals.

- Large percent differences may be due to noise.

- Small percent differences may represent signals.

- There are usually several ways to measure most processes.

- Eight or more successive values on the same side of the central line is interpreted as a signal.

- Tables of values overwhelm the user with extraneous detail.

- Graphs reveal interesting structures present in the data.

- Passing data through a computer does not remove problems which may exist with the data themselves.

- Monthly management reports are an impoverished way to communicate numerical values.

- Arbitrary numerical goals tend to distort the system more than they transform it.

- The Voice of the Customer defines what you want from a system.

- The Voice of the Process defines what you will get from a system.

- It is management's job to work to bring the Voice of the Process into alignment with the Voice of the Customer.

- The key to the successful use of process behavior charts is the practice of the way of thinking which goes with them.

FIVE

BUT YOU HAVE TO USE THE RIGHT DATA

Without meaningful data there can be no meaningful analysis. The interpretation of any data set must be based upon the context of those data.

Unfortunately, much of the data reported to executives today are aggregated and summed over so many different operating units and processes that they cannot be said to have any context except a historical one—they were all collected during the same time period. While this may be rational with monetary figures, it can be devastating to other types of data.

ON - TIME CLOSINGS OF ACCOUNTS

Each month the accounting department closes and reconciles the books for each of the departments in the plant. The number of manhours required for each departmental closing is recorded. If a closing requires fewer than 65 manhours, it is said to be completed "on-time." If a closing requires more than 65 manhours, then it is not completed "on-time." The accounting manager has set a goal of 95% on-time closings. (Notice that this is a goal on meeting a goal!)

The percentage of on-time closings is routinely included in the monthly report.

		Monthly Report for July							
		July	Monthly		% Diff	Year-to-Date Values			This YTD as
		Actual	Plan	%	from July	Total or		%	% Diff. of
Operations:	Dept	Value	Value	Diff	Last Yr	Average	Plan	Diff	Last YTD
On-Time Closings of Accounts (%)	06	74.3	95	−21.8	−23.5	87.8	95	−7.6	−2.7

Figure 5.1: On-Time Closings of Accounts

Once again, the monthly report does not provide an adequate context for anyone to fully understand and interpret the data presented. The number of departments, out of 35, whose books were closed "on-time" is recorded each month. These values for the past 31 months are shown in Figure 5.2.

				Numbers of On-Time Closings							
Year	Jan	Feb	Mar	Apr	May	Jun	Jul	Aug	Sep	Oct	Nov	Dec
One	32	30	32	33	32	28	30	31	32	32	32	33
Two	29	31	32	33	31	31	34	30	33	28	33	34
Three	33	33	31	29	33	30	26					

Figure 5.2: Numbers of On-Time Closings (Out of 35 Closings per Month)

Every count has an area of opportunity. Here the area of opportunity is the number of closings each month. If the area of opportunity remains constant over time, then you may directly compare the counts. If the area of opportunity changes from month to month, then you will have to convert the *counts* into *rates* before comparing the month-to-month values. With the on-time closings data the area of opportunity remains constant, so you may work with the counts or you may work with the percentages—the charts will tell the same story either way.

The current value of 26 (shown as 74.3% in Figure 5.1) is the lowest on record. Is it a signal that something has changed, or is it simply a low value which is part of the routine variation?

The simplest way to answer this question is to use a process behavior chart. The *XmR* chart[13] for the number of on-time closings is shown in

---

13 For those who expected a *p*-chart see note on page 138.

Figure 5.3. The limits on this chart are based on the values from the first two years. The average number of on-time closings is 31.5. The Average Moving Range is 2.0. There is no meaningful Upper Natural Process Limit, since the maximum count is 35. The Lower Natural Process Limit is 26.2. The Upper Range Limit is 6.5.

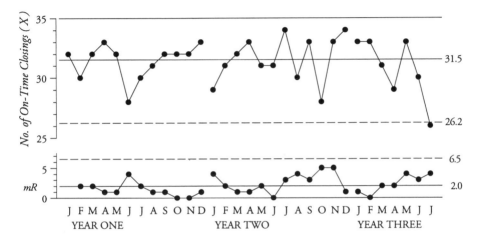

Figure 5.3: XmR Chart for the Number of On-Time Closings of Accounts

The last point on the X-chart is the current value. It falls below the lower limit and is therefore taken to be a signal. Something was different about the closings in July of this year—detectably fewer departments had their books closed on time. The process behavior chart does not tell us what happened, but it does tell us that something did happen and that some questions are in order.

However, with the exception of the July value, the on-time closings behave predictably. Up until the present, they have averaged 31.5 on-time closings per month (90% on-time). This means that while they might occasionally have a month with better than 95% on-time closings, they cannot average 95% on-time. This goal is beyond the capability of the system. In order to have an average which will meet this goal the system will have to be changed in some basic way.

Charting the on-time percentage will not reveal how to change the system—it will not highlight the problem areas. The accounting manager will not be able to bring about the desired changes by setting goals for the on-time percentage. Instead of jawboning the *people*, the manager will have to work on improving the *system*.

Summary counts and percentages, such as these on-time data, will never be focused and specific. They are too highly accumulated. At best such accumulations may serve as report cards. However, because the wrong things may be counted, or the right counts may be accumulated in the wrong way, some accumulated measures will not even yield useful report cards.

With the on-time closings, the key to useful data comes from the realization that the closing of the books may well involve different operations and procedures for each of the 35 departments. Therefore, some departmental books may well take longer to close than others. This means that you will need to consider the 35 closings as 35 parallel operations, each with its own stream of data—the number of manhours needed each month. These 35 data streams will need to be analyzed separately in order to discover if they behave predictably or not.

If a given departmental closing displays predictable variation, then it will do no good to set a goal on the number of manhours for that closing—you will only get what the system will deliver and setting a goal can only distort the system. Goals are one of the greatest causes of creativity!

If a given departmental closing does not display predictable variation, then there is again no point in setting a goal—the system has no well-defined capability so there is no way of knowing just what the system will produce.

Instead of setting arbitrary goals, the accounting manager needs to analyze the data for the departmental closings in order to discover problem areas and opportunities for improvement.

Much of the managerial data in use today consists of aggregated counts. Such data tend to be virtually useless in identifying the nature of problems. (The aggregation destroys the context of the individual counts.) The work of process improvement requires specific measures and contextual knowledge. These characteristics are more readily available from measures of activity than from counts of events.

Measures of actual activity will generally be more useful than simple counts of how many times a goal has been met. When management is serious about improvement they will have to take the time to develop measures that help, instead of simply counting the good days and the bad days. In order to develop appropriate measures, the teams need to look back at their process and find the variables that best represent their process. Thus, good data do not occur by accident. They have to be obtained by plan.

HOT METAL

This example shows how a paucity of data, coupled with departmental pressures to reduce costs, can result in huge losses.

"Hot metal" is hauled from the blast furnace to the steel furnace by means of special railroad cars. When the cars are ready to leave the blast furnace the operator calls the steel furnace to let them know that the hot metal is on its way. The steel furnace operator then begins to melt 200 tons of cold charge so that it will be up to temperature when the hot metal arrives. This meltdown proceeds on the assumption that the hot metal will be in the steel furnace ladle house some 20 minutes after the tap at the blast furnace was completed. Any delay in this delivery of the hot metal will result in wasted energy—the cold charge will have been melted too soon, and it will have to be held at an elevated temperature while waiting for the hot metal.

Delays are hurting productivity. "Waiting for hot metal" is the most common notation in the steel furnace logbook. Therefore, a team headed by the steel furnace superintendent decided to collect some data on the transit time for the delivery of hot metal. For one month they recorded the time that each tap was completed at the blast furnace, and the time that the railcar arrived in the steel furnace ladle house. The difference between these two times was the delivery time.

At the team meeting copies of the transit time log sheet—a full page of numbers and dates—were passed around. One engineer who had "analyzed the data" reported that the "average transit time was about 60 minutes, with a standard deviation of about 30 minutes." Everyone looked at the log sheets for about 30 seconds, nodded and started looking at the next item on the agenda. The traditional analysis by osmosis was over.

The author interrupted at this point and began to pass out copies of the histogram of the transit times. Before 10 copies could be passed around, the superintendent of the steel furnace observed, "There are two things going on here!"

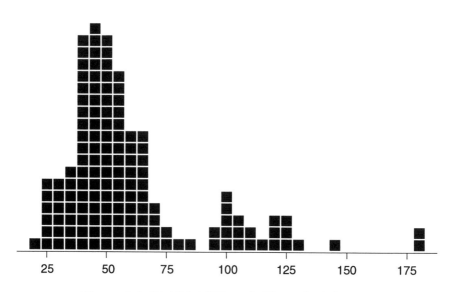

Figure 5.4: Hot Metal Transit Times in Minutes

At this comment, and with the evidence in their hands, everyone in the room turned to the general foreman for transportation who was both figuratively and literally sitting in the corner. He looked at the histogram for a moment, and then said, "The only way they can take over 100 minutes to travel one mile is to unhook and go do another job before delivering the hot metal."

The transportation manager had assigned only one railroad crew per shift to service a large section of the plant. This one crew had to respond to all the transportation needs in that section as best they could. After all, the transportation department had to hold its costs down. The transportation manager was evaluated on how well he did in cutting his costs. So even though the fuel costs for the steel furnace for *one* 10 minute delay would equal the cost of a train crew for 24 hours, nobody was counting this fuel cost against the transportation manager. It didn't show up in his budget.

But not all of the problem was in the transportation department. While the hot metal could be delivered in 20 minutes, the histogram suggests that it is a bit optimistic to plan on a 20 minute delivery (they did it one time in this sequence of 141 deliveries). Plan for a 20 minute delivery, and virtually every heat will be delayed, and many of them will be delayed by far more than 10 minutes.

The morals of this story are several:

(1) optimization of the parts does not equal optimization of the whole;

(2) traditional cost accounting can hide or miss the essential figures;

(3) analysis by osmosis is very ineffective;

(4) graphs communicate the essence of the data better than tables; and

(5) it is dangerous to confuse a target value with the Voice of the Process.

MATERIAL COSTS

This example tells the story of a traditional improvement effort. It considers several different measures of activity together. As before, the monthly report format for presenting results had obscured the big picture. The use of process behavior charts will allow us to collect the multiple strands together and gain the needed perspective.

At one time Department 13 had material costs which amounted to 75 percent of their production costs. During what we shall call Year One, a project team was formed and given the job of reducing the material costs in Department 13.

During August of Year One, a process change was made which was designed to reduce the material utilization. Following this change the average material cost per 100 pounds of material dropped from $215.22 to $208.20.

During March of Year Two, another process modification was implemented. During the next four months the material cost dropped to an average of $205.37 per 100 pounds produced.

In July of Year Two a change was made in the formulation of the material used in Department 13. This change resulted in an average material cost of $201.22 per 100 pounds produced. One month later the project team and Department 13 got an award for these successful cost reductions.

Finally, in January of Year Three, Department 13 changed suppliers for some of their raw materials. This resulted in an average material cost of $198.46 per 100 pounds produced.

Against this background, the monthly report for July of Year Three showed the following values for Department 13.

Production:	Dept	July Actual Value	Monthly Plan Value	% Diff	% Diff from July Last Yr	Year-to-Date Values Total or Average	Plan	% Diff	This YTD as % Diff. of Last YTD
						Monthly Report for July			
Production Volume (1000's lbs)	13	34.5	36.	−4.2	−2.0	251.5	252	−0.2	−8.0
Material Costs ($/100 lbs)	13	198.29	201.22	−1.5	−1.9	198.46	201.22	−1.4	−3.6
Manhours per 100 lbs	13	4.45	4.16	+7.0	+4.5	4.46	4.16	+7.2	+9.3
Energy & Fixed Costs / 100 lbs	13	11.34	11.27	+0.6	+11.3	11.02	11.27	−2.2	+9.2
Total Production Costs/100 lbs	13	280.83	278.82	+0.7	+0.9	280.82	278.82	+0.7	+0.4

Figure 5.5: Monthly Report for Department 13

Production volume is down four percent from the monthly target. It is also down two percent from last year. The year-to-date value is pretty much in line with the yearly plan value, but it is eight percent below last year.

Year-to-date material costs are down almost four percent from a year ago, which is good. For this year as a whole, manhours are up nine percent from last year, which is bad. Energy and fixed costs are up, which surprises no one.

Total production costs are essentially unchanged from last year, which is good, especially in light of the *increases* in manhours, energy, and fixed costs.

In all, it is a rather mixed bag of results—some good news, some bad news, some neutral results. Each of the five categories used in the management report will be considered as a separate time series on the following pages. Of course, the complete story is a composite of all of these time series, but we have to assemble the big picture one piece at a time.

We shall begin with the material cost values.

Material Costs Per 100 Pounds											
Year	Jan	Feb	Mar	Apr	May	Jun	Jul	Aug	Sep	Oct	Nov	Dec
One	214.79	215.22	214.79	214.36	216.51	213.71	216.79	216.08	208.34	208.76	206.67	208.34
Two	210.43	206.67	206.13	206.13	205.11	204.09	202.09	201.89	201.69	201.49	201.09	199.09
Three	198.69	197.89	198.09	199.68	198.88	197.70	198.29					

Figure 5.6: Material Costs for Department 13

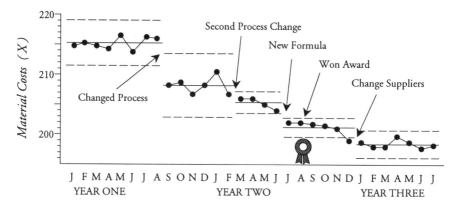

Figure 5.7: X-Charts for Material Costs

The material costs are shown in Figure 5.7. The gaps in the record correspond to the changes made by the project team. The effectiveness of these changes can clearly and easily be seen on this graph.

The limits shown with each segment are the Natural Process Limits for individual values. The moving ranges used to obtain these limits are not shown in the interest of keeping the graph from becoming too busy. By comparing the *limits* for one segment with the *running record* of another segment you can see that the changes made by the project team did result in definite and real reductions in the material costs.

				Manhours Per 100 Pounds							
Year	Jan	Feb	Mar	Apr	May	Jun	Jul	Aug	Sep	Oct	Nov	Dec
One	3.87	3.86	3.90	3.93	3.92	3.86	3.92	3.90	4.02	3.95	4.01	3.95
Two	4.01	4.00	4.06	4.10	4.07	4.09	4.26	4.24	4.27	4.24	4.26	4.29
Three	4.43	4.45	4.47	4.47	4.51	4.43	4.45					

Figure 5.8: Manhours for Department 13

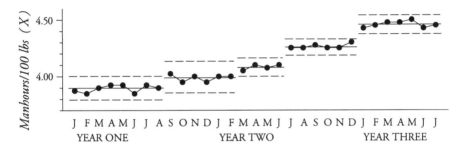

Figure 5.9: *X*-Charts for Manhours Per 100 Pounds

The manhours per 100 pounds of product are shown in Figure 5.9. The gaps in the record correspond to the changes made by the project team. The limits for each segment were computed using the moving ranges for that segment, even though the moving range charts are not shown in this figure.

The graph in Figure 5.9 shows that there have been increases in the number of manhours per 100 pounds of product. *Each and every change made by the project team had the effect of increasing the actual labor content of the product.*

The small amount of month-to-month variation in this time series makes it easy to interpret this graph. Placing Natural Process Limits on each segment just makes it clearer that these incremental increases are real.

The production volumes are shown in Figure 5.11. The gaps in the record correspond to the changes made by the project team. The limits shown were computed from the first eight values and their moving

				Production Volumes (thousands of pounds)								
Year	Jan	Feb	Mar	Apr	May	Jun	Jul	Aug	Sep	Oct	Nov	Dec
One	39.1	38.7	38.8	39.7	42.3	43.3	42.0	44.4	42.3	41.3	36.9	38.3
Two	40.1	40.4	36.5	41.8	40.5	39.1	35.2	37.5	34.7	39.7	37.9	36.4
Three	39.1	36.0	35.5	34.6	36.8	35.0	34.5					

Figure 5.10: Production Volumes for Department 13

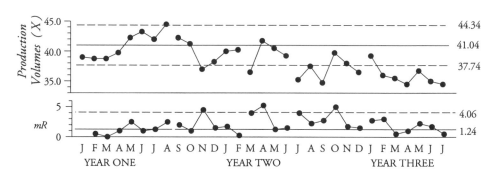

Figure 5.11: *XmR* Chart for Production Volumes

ranges. The first eight values suggest an upward trend for the production volumes. However, following the first process change, and continuing through the subsequent changes, there is a downward trend in the production volume. In addition to the two large transition ranges, the moving range chart shows three other points above the limit. These three values suggest three additional changes in the level of production in Department 13. If these were deliberate changes made by management, then there is no need to look for assignable causes. If these changes were surprises, then there is something to be gained by looking for the assignable causes behind these shifts.

Thus, the production volumes are down while the manhours per 100 pounds are up—*a classic description of declining productivity—totally buried in the figures in the Monthly Report.*

					Energy and Fixed Costs (per 100 pounds)						
Year	Jan	Feb	Mar	Apr	May	Jun	Jul	Aug	Sep	Oct	Nov	Dec
One	8.96	9.08	8.97	9.25	9.50	9.12	9.21	9.32	9.44	9.60	9.82	9.75
Two	9.74	9.96	10.02	10.05	10.34	10.32	10.19	10.19	10.33	10.57	10.87	10.33
Three	10.82	10.61	10.92	11.12	11.18	11.16	11.34					

Figure 5.12: Energy and Fixed Costs for Department 13

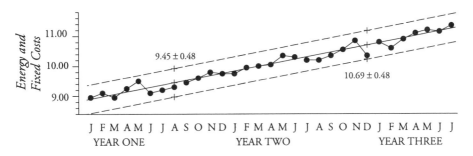

Figure 5.13: Trended *XmR* Chart for Energy and Fixed Costs

The energy and fixed costs are shown in Figure 5.13. The gaps in the record correspond to the changes made by the project team.

The energy and fixed costs have risen as expected. In fact, the running record shows a fairly straight line sloping upward. Note the difference between this graph and the graph for manhours per 100 pounds. The slope of the points extends across the gaps. There is no suggestion of a step increase at the gaps like there was with the manhours data.

The sloping central line was obtained by connecting the average of the first 15 values with the average of the last 15 values. The average of the first 15 values was plotted above August of Year One, while the average of the last 15 values was plotted above December of Year Two. The limits were then placed around this sloping line in the same manner that they would be placed around a horizontal central line, based on an Average Moving Range of 0.18.

Total Production Costs
(per 100 pounds)

Year	Jan	Feb	Mar	Apr	May	Jun	Jul	Aug	Sep	Oct	Nov	Dec
One	281.80	282.80	282.26	282.56	284.81	280.73	284.30	283.90	278.08	277.61	276.64	277.34
Two	282.33	282.39	279.08	279.73	278.54	277.81	278.31	277.80	278.21	277.78	277.99	275.92
Three	280.39	279.70	280.53	282.32	282.22	279.74	280.83					

Figure 5.14: Total Production Costs for Department 13

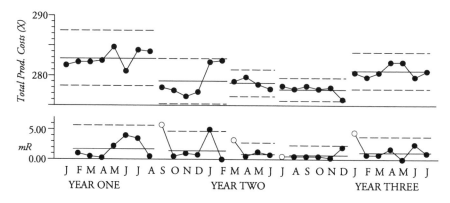

Figure 5.15: *XmR* Charts for Total Production Costs per 100 Pounds

The total production costs are shown in Figure 5.15. The gaps in the record correspond to the changes made by the project team. The limits shown were based upon each segment, ignoring the moving ranges shown in white (which represent the four known changes).

The first process change resulted in a definite drop in the total production cost, although inflation of other costs had eroded these gains by the first two months of Year Two. The second process change caused a slight drop in the total production cost. Finally, even though the final change at the beginning of Year Three did reduce the material cost, the increases in the other costs have offset this gain. Still, all in all, they are doing better than they were at the beginning of Year One, or at least it would appear that way from these data.

While the total cost data and the material cost data look good, and the energy costs look pretty much like they should look, there are some indications of trouble in the time series for manhours and production volumes. All of these measures are computed for Department 13. Unfortunately, Department 13 does not use its own stuff, and therefore it has no way of assessing the quality of its product.

The figures developed from the records in Department 13 cannot take the quality of the product into account. This makes all of the cost figures suspect, because they are based on pounds shipped, not pounds converted into usable product in Department 14.

Department 14, on the other hand, keeps careful track of their successful conversion rate. Among the problems that can occur in Department 14, the major cause of scrap is "will not mould." The category has been shown to be most directly affected by the quality of the component supplied by Department 13.

The percentages of scrap (by weight) due to "will not mould" are shown in Figure 5.16, and the values are plotted in Figure 5.17.

Percentage of Material Lost Due to "Will Not Mould"											
Year	Jan	Feb	Mar	Apr	May	Jun	Jul	Aug	Sep	Oct	Nov	Dec
One	2.7	2.0	1.6	1.8	2.1	2.7	1.6	2.4	4.5	4.0	2.9	3.4
Two	4.5	4.3	7.7	7.2	8.4	6.3	11.3	10.8	10.5	12.8	9.8	11.9
Three	16.3	17.6	14.6	15.5	17.9	15.8	14.8					

Figure 5.16: Scrap Percentages for Department 14

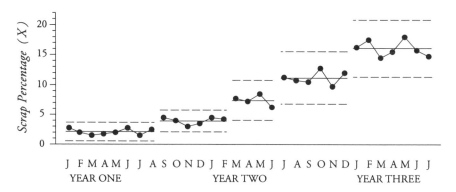

Figure 5.17: *X*-**Charts for Scrap Percentages for Department 14**

The Natural Process Limits are shown for each segment in Figure 5.17. While each segment stays within its own set of limits, each segment, beginning with September of Year One, has points that fall outside the preceding set of limits. This means that each and every signal in these data correspond to one of the changes made by the project team in Department 13.

This negative impact of the project team's efforts was not seen because of the artificial boundary created by the "departments" and the subsequent partitioning of the management data. While everyone was minding their own department, no one was minding the store.

If we delete the pounds of scrap produced in Department 14 from the total amount of product produced in Department 13, then the data for Department 13 will tell a different story. We begin by taking the total production costs and scaling them to reflect the scrap rate due to "will not mould."

			Honest (Actual) Production Costs									
			(per 100 pounds of usable product)									
Year	Jan	Feb	Mar	Apr	May	Jun	Jul	Aug	Sep	Oct	Nov	Dec
One	289.62	287.96	286.85	287.74	290.92	288.52	288.92	290.88	291.18	289.18	284.90	287.10
Two	295.63	295.08	302.36	301.43	304.08	296.49	313.77	311.44	310.85	318.56	308.19	313.19
Three	334.99	339.44	328.49	334.11	343.75	332.2	329.61					

Figure 5.18: Honest Production Costs for Department 13

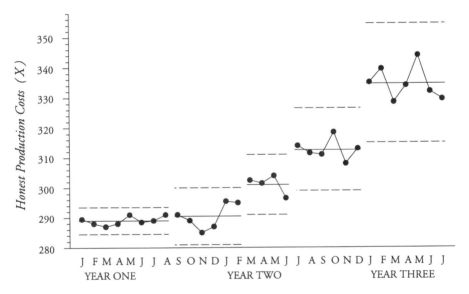

Figure 5.19: X-Charts for Honest Production Costs for Department 13

Figure 5.19 shows the net value to the company of the changes made by the project team in Department 13. They effectively increased the total cost of the finished product every time they made a change, and they got an award for doing it! One cannot help but recall Dr. Deming's first theorem : *"No one gives a hoot about profits—if they did they would be interested in learning better ways to make them."*

What if the changes had not been made? What if Department 13 had done nothing? The total cost per 100 pounds of usable product may be estimated as follows. Assume that Department 13 continued to use the same process, with the same supplier, and without the modifications in material usage or formulation. Assume material costs go up five percent each year. Allow for the increases in wages and the increases in energy costs which are known to have occurred. Assume that the scrap rate in Department 14 averages the 2.1 percent shown by the first eight months of Year One, and assume that the labor content of the product stays the same as it was at the beginning of Year One. These conditions will result in the estimated total production costs shown in Figures 5.20 and 5.21.

The company would have come out ahead if they had kept the production system which was in place at the beginning of Year One and sent the project team for a two-year, expense-paid vacation in Cuba.

The second tragedy of this story is that the managers had too much invested in the "improvement" effort to admit that it had been a failure. Therefore, the messenger who revealed the effect of all these "process improvements" soon took a job at another company.

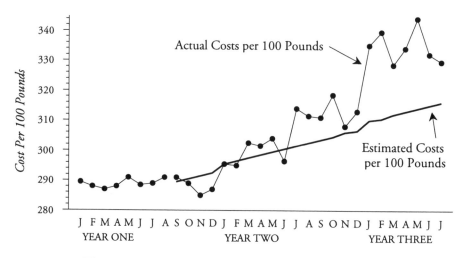

Figure 5.20: Actual Costs versus Estimated Costs

				Estimated Total Production Costs (per 100 pounds of usable product)								
Year	Jan	Feb	Mar	Apr	May	Jun	Jul	Aug	Sep	Oct	Nov	Dec
One	289.62	287.96	286.85	287.74	290.92	288.52	288.92	290.88	289.26	290.35	291.48	292.34
Two	295.25	296.40	297.41	298.38	299.61	300.54	301.36	302.31	303.41	304.62	305.89	306.31
Three	309.78	310.54	311.85	313.04	314.09	315.07	316.25					

Figure 5.21: Estimated Production Costs for Department 13

There are several morals to this story.

- A manager must look at the whole picture, not just the narrow slices provided by the departmental figures. The artificial boundaries created by departments can distort both the data and the system.

- Good accounting practices for a whole company may be inappropriate when applied on a departmental level. Trying to micromanage and microaccount can result in severe distortions of the data.

- When it comes to pleasing our customers, the important figures are often unknown and unknowable. It is dangerous to run a company using only the visible figures.

- Some figures have the seeds of distortion built in. One transportation department was tracking the "transportation utilization efficiency." If someone decided to make this number look better, they could simply wait until they had full loads before shipping any product. Of course this would have a negative impact upon the figures for on-time shipments and would result in unhappy customers, but it would certainly make the utilization numbers look good.

- The optimization of each department will always result in a plant which is suboptimal. The optimization of the whole system will require that some departments be operated suboptimally. However, by encouraging competition between managers, most organizations make it impossible for departments to cooperate for the good of the company.

SPILLS

This example is more complex than the preceding examples because it discusses how to transform counts of rare events into useful measures of activity. It will be of greatest interest to those who have to work with the counts of very rare events. Others may wish to skip to the next chapter.

Department 16 has occasional spills. They are not desirable, and everything possible is done to prevent them. Of course, when a spill does occur it has to be handled in a specific manner, and the clean-up has to be properly documented. In the past they have averaged one spill every eight months. The most recent spill was on July 13. The monthly report showed this spill in the following manner.

		July Actual Value	Monthly Average Value	% Diff	Diff from July Last Yr	Total	Average	% Diff	This YTD as % Diff. of Last YTD
	Dept								
Safety:									
Spills	16	1	0.125	+ 700	+ 1	2	0.875	+ 129	+ 100

Monthly Report for July / **Year-to-Date Values**

Figure 5.22: Spills in Department 16

We should note that a single spill is 700% above average. When dealing with very small numbers, such as the counts of rare events, a one unit change can result in a huge percentage difference. The rest of the "information" shown on this line of the monthly report is virtually useless.

Once again, the appropriate perspective is provided by a time series graph, as seen in Figure 5.23.

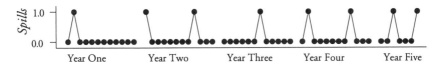

Figure 5.23: Time Series for Spills in Department 16

Given the extreme simplicity of these data, a table of values is redundant. Figure 5.23 shows the data from the past four years, plus the data for this current year.

When you are working with count data and the average count drops below 1.0 per time period (or per sample) the *XmR* chart is inappropriate. Counts for rare events have to be placed on a process behavior chart by means of other charting techniques.

The usual process behavior chart for these data would be the chart which is commonly called a *c*-chart. This chart uses slightly different formulas than the *XmR* chart, and these formulas are justified by the fact that these data are the counts of rare events which occur independently of each other. The *c*-chart will also require areas of opportunity which are approximately equal from time period to time period.

For a *c*-chart you must compute an average count. During the first four years shown there were a total of six spills. Six spills in 48 months gives an average of:

$$\bar{X} = \frac{6 \text{ spills}}{48 \text{ months}} = 0.125 \text{ spills per month}$$

The average will be the central line for the *c*-chart, and the upper limit will be computed according to the formula:

$$UCL_C = \bar{X} + 3\sqrt{\bar{X}} = 0.125 + 3\sqrt{0.125} = 1.186$$

The *c*-chart is shown in Figure 5.24. In spite of the fact that a single spill is 700 percent above the average, the *c*-chart does not show any points outside the limits. This is not a problem with the charts, but rather a problem with the data themselves. Counts of rare events are inherently insensitive and weak. No matter how these counts are analyzed, there is nothing to discover here.

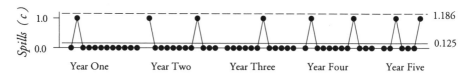

Figure 5.24: *c*-Chart for Spills

Yet there are other ways to characterize the spills. Instead of *counting* the number of spills each year, you could instead *measure* the number of days between the spills. For the first four years the time intervals between the spills are computed as follows.

Spills in Department 16								
Date of Spill	2/23/01	1/11/02	9/15/02	7/6/03	2/19/04	9/29/04	3/20/05	7/13/05
Day of Year	54	11	258	188	50	272	79	194
Days Between Spills		322	247	295	227	222	172	115

Figure 5.25: Dates of Spills in Department 16

One spill in 332 days converts into a spill rate of:

$$\frac{1 \text{ spill}}{322 \text{ days}} = 0.0031 \text{ spills per day}$$

Multiplying the daily spill rate by 365 gives a yearly spill rate.

(0.0031 spills per day) x (365 days per year) = 1.13 spills per year.

Thus, the interval between the first and second spills is equivalent to having 1.13 spills per year. Continuing in this manner, the intervals between the first six spills are converted into five instantaneous spill rates (in spills per year). These five spill rates and the accompanying moving ranges are shown in Figure 5.26.

The average spill rate during the first four years is thus 1.42 spills per year. The Average Moving Range is 0.2475. Using these values we obtain the *XmR* chart shown in Figure 5.27.

		Spill Rates				
Days Between Spills		322	247	295	227	222
Spills per Day		0.0031	0.0040	0.0034	0.0044	0.0045
Spills per Year	X	1.13	1.48	1.24	1.61	1.64
moving ranges	mR		0.35	0.24	0.37	0.03

Figure 5.26: Spill Rates for Department 16

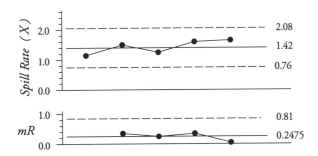

Figure 5.27: *XmR* Chart for Spill Rates

The two spills in the current year had intervals of 172 days and 115 days respectively. These intervals convert into spill rates of 2.12 spills per year and 3.17 spills per year. When these values are added to the *XmR* chart the result is Figure 5.28.

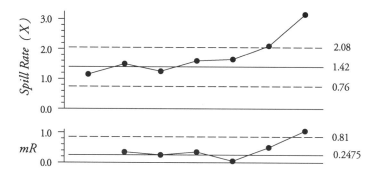

Figure 5.28: Complete *XmR* Chart for Spill Rates

The first spill in the current year is above the upper Natural Process Limit. Thus, this spill signals an increase in the spill rate.

The second spill in the current year is above the upper limit, and it corresponds to a moving range that is also above the limit, suggesting a further increase in the spill rate.

Both of these signals need to be investigated. Both of them are missed by the *c*-chart approach.

In general, *counts are weaker than measurements*. Counts of rare events are no exception. When possible, it will always be more satisfactory to *measure the activity* than to merely *count events*. And, as shown in this example, the times between undesirable events are best charted as rates. This inversion allows the chart to detect a deterioration more easily than would be the case if the times themselves were charted.

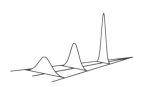

SUMMARY

- As data are aggregated they lose their context and their usefulness.

- Aggregated data may be used as a report card, but they will not pinpoint what needs to be fixed.

- Setting goals does nothing to change the system.

- Setting goals on meeting goals is an act of desperation.

- Counts are weaker than measurements.

- Measures of activity will produce more insight than counts of how many times something has happened.

- Some measures have the seeds of distortion built in.

- When it comes to pleasing our customers, the important figures are often unknown and unknowable.

- Narrowly focused improvement efforts can be destructive.

SIX

LOOK WHAT YOU'VE BEEN MISSING

Data are collected as a basis for action. Yet before anyone can use data as a basis for action the data have to be interpreted. The proper interpretation of data will require that the data be presented in context, and that the analysis technique used will filter out the noise.

The traditional approach of using percent differences to provide a context for interpreting a single value is like using the graph shown in Figure 6.1. Have things gotten better, worse, or stayed the same?

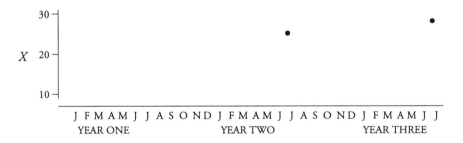

Figure 6.1: An Executive Time Series

Limited comparisons of pairs of values, such as the percent difference values, may occasionally be of use, but they do not present a broad enough context to always point toward the proper action. Moreover, they do not attempt to filter out any noise.

Likewise, comparisons to specifications, plans, goals, targets, budgets, or averages, do not attempt to filter out any noise. These comparisons simply try to characterize whether you are "operating okay" or are "in trouble." If you are in trouble, these comparisons offer no suggestion about how to get out of trouble. If you are operating okay, these comparisons do not predict if you are likely to continue to operate okay. These comparisons only attempt to characterize the recent past.

Graphs are the most powerful tool available for presenting data in context. Among the many graphs possible, the running record and the histogram are the two most useful. In fact, it is the running record which is the basis for the process behavior charts.

Process behavior charts are the simplest way of filtering out the probable noise in any data set. These charts will allow you to concentrate on any signals which may be present in the data, while ignoring the background noise.

Hopefully, these statements have been demonstrated in the preceding chapters. However, if you are still skeptical, let us return to the in-process inventory data and consider the alternative.

In November of Year One, the in-process inventory value was at an all-time low of 15. Consider just how a manager might have responded to this value. What if the manager had decided to present an award to Department 17 in honor of the low value for November? He could have had a nice ceremony in the company cafeteria, with cake and cookies for all. Every one could be proud of what they had achieved.

Figure 6.2: Time Series Graph for the In-Process Inventory

Then, as the in-process inventory increased in each of the next three months, the manager would have repented of ever issuing the award. It would seem to have been counter productive. Instead of holding the in-process inventory down, the folks in Department 17 would seem to have gotten lazy, and the in-process inventory shot right back up to where it was before.

Figure 6.3: More In-Process Inventory Values

At this point the manager might well decide to change his strategy—no more Mr. Nice Guy. What this group needs is a tough manager.

Figure 6.4: 19 Months of In-Process Inventories

So, in July of Year Two, when the in-process inventory hits a value of 25, the manager swings into high gear. He calls everybody in and reads them the riot act. He demands that they do something to keep the in-process inventories down. Following this tantrum, the personnel of Department 17 keep a low profile. Short of hiding material in the dark corners of the plant they don't know how to reduce the in-process inventory. So they hold their breath and hope the inventory levels will drop.

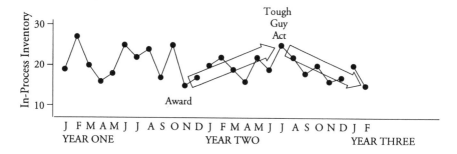

Figure 6.5: 26 Months of In-Process Inventories

And what is the boss likely to think about all this? He gave this department an award and then he watched things get worse. Then he read them riot act and watched things get better. While nothing was done to change the system during the past seven months, the manger is still likely to decide that the recent "improvements" are due to his intervention in July of Year Two. Obviously Pharaoh was right! Tough management works!

What is wrong with both of these conclusions about what works and what doesn't work? Both are examples of superstitious learning. Both are based on the interpretation of the high values and low values as signals. However, as the process behavior chart in Figure 6.6 clearly and plainly shows, *none of these individual values were signals.*

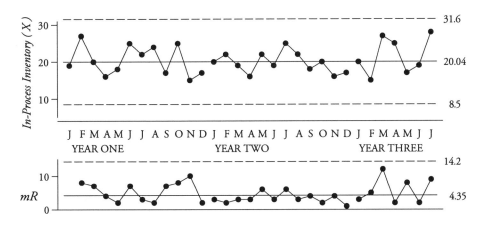

Figure 6.6: *XmR* Chart for the In-Process Inventory

While the numerical values are different from month to month, they all represent the same underlying system. The high values do not represent anything different than do the low values. They should all be interpreted alike. Interpreting the low value as indicative of good performance was an example of interpreting noise as if it were a signal. Interpreting the high value as indicative of poor performance is also an example of interpreting noise as if it were a signal. Both interpretations are completely wrong. Both lead to the wrong actions, and both mistakes mislead the manager in his understanding of what has happened.

Unfortunately, most managers are proud of their ability to interpret noise as if it were a signal. They consider this to be an art.

No matter how eloquent the explanation, no matter how convincing the logic, noise is still noise. Any attempt to explain noise is merely an exercise in wishful thinking—the result is pure fiction which will have no contact with reality.

Process behavior charts are the simplest way to filter out the noise which is present in all data sets. The failure to use process behavior charts to analyze time series is one of the best ways known to man to increase costs, waste effort, and lower morale.

LESSONS

I. **Data have no meaning apart from their context.**

Data presented without a context are effectively rendered meaningless. Monthly reports do not typically provide an adequate context.

II. **Before you can interpret data you must have a method of analysis.**

a. **Comparisons to specifications, goals, and targets** do not provide a rational context for analysis nor do they encourage constancy of purpose. They encourage a binary world view in which you are either "operating okay" or are "in trouble." These comparisons do not allow you to separate potential signals from probable noise. They literally do not consider the impact of variation upon the data. They simply ignore variation and treat every fluctuation as a signal.

b. **Comparisons to average values** are only slightly better than comparisons to specifications. Here the process or outcome is characterized as being either "above average" or "below average." These comparisons do not allow you to separate potential signals from probable noise. They literally do not consider the impact of variation upon the data. They simply ignore variation and treat every fluctuation as a signal.

c. **Process behavior charts** provide a better approach to the analysis of data. They overcome the shortcomings of the other approaches because they explicitly consider the effects of variation upon the data. By characterizing all variation as either routine (which is predictable) or as exceptional (and therefore unpredictable) the process behavior chart shifts the emphasis away from the results and toward the behavior of the system which produced the results. This shift in emphasis is a major step on the road of continual improvement.

When a system is predictable, it is already performing as consistently as possible. Looking for assignable causes is a waste of time and effort. Instead, you can meaningfully work on making improvements and modifications to the process.

When a system is unpredictable, it will be futile to try and improve or modify the process. Instead you must seek to identify the assignable causes which affect the system.

The failure to distinguish between these two different courses of action is a major source of confusion and wasted effort in business today.

III. **While all data contain noise, some data contain signals.**
Before you can detect a signal, you must filter out the noise.
There have been many different statistical techniques invented to separate potential signals from probable noise. Of all of these techniques the process behavior chart is the easiest to use.

IV. **The purpose of analysis is insight.**
The best analysis is the simplest analysis which provides the needed insight. When the process behavior chart is used in conjunction with histograms, flow charts, cause and effect diagrams, Pareto charts, and running records, it is possible to obtain from the data those insights which will remain hidden from those who continue to use the traditional analyses.

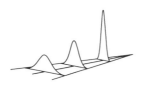

WHAT SHOULD YOU DO NOW?

Statistics has never been a spectator sport. Process behavior charts are no exception. You should see if you can compute the limits and construct an *XmR* chart.

1. The U.S. Trade Deficits for the last half of 1988 are shown in Figure 6.7. Use the data of Figure 6.7, and the blank form in Figure 6.8 to plot the time series graph for the U.S. Trade Deficits for the last half of 1988.

	Jul	Aug	Sep	Oct	Nov	Dec
1988	10.5	11.2	9.2	10.1	10.4	10.5

Figure 6.7: Monthly U.S. Trade Deficits, 1988 ($ billions)

2. Use the data in Figure 6.7 to compute the monthly moving ranges. Note that moving ranges are defined to be positive values, and are found by computing the differences between successive values. Write these values in the space provided in Figure 6.8, and plot the running record of the moving ranges.
3. Compute the average trade deficit for the last half of 1988.
4. Compute the Average Moving Range.
5. Compute the Natural Process Limits for the *X*-chart using the formulas on page 60 or on page 137.
6. Compute the Upper Range Limit using the formula on page 60 or on page 137.

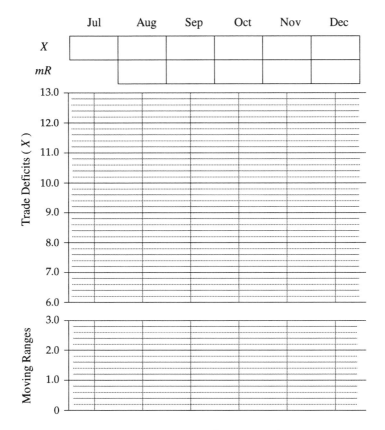

Figure 6.8: Form for *XmR* Chart

7. Plot the *limits* from Figure 6.8 on Figure 6.10.
8. The U.S. Trade Deficits for the first half of 1989 are shown on the next page in Figure 6.9. Plot these values and their moving ranges on the form given in Figure 6.10.

	Jan	Feb	Mar	Apr	May	Jun
1989	8.7	8.7	7.0	6.8	9.6	9.0

Figure 6.9: Monthly U.S. Trade Deficits, 1989 ($ billions)

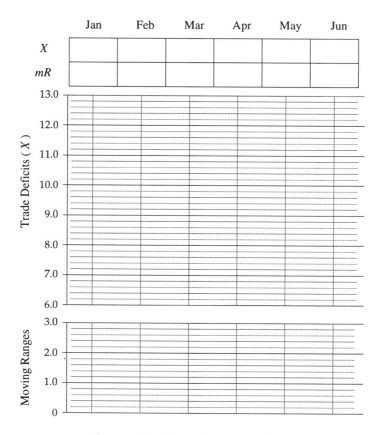

Figure 6.10: Form for *XmR* Chart

There are two indications of shifts in Figure 6.10. The first shift was favorable, and the second was unfavorable.

9. When is this favorable shift *detected*?
10. When might this favorable shift have begun?
11. When is the unfavorable shift detected?

THE TRANSFORMATION

There is an obstacle on the path from awareness to understanding.[14] In order to move beyond awareness, you must first begin to practice the use of these techniques. It is only after you use these tools that you begin to understand just how they work and why they work. Once this understanding has taken root you can begin to actually explain the phenomena revealed by the tools. This feedback cycle continues and becomes the new way of thinking which is the basis for continual improvement. In short, you must first act—in order to understand—in order to explain— in order to be able to act effectively.

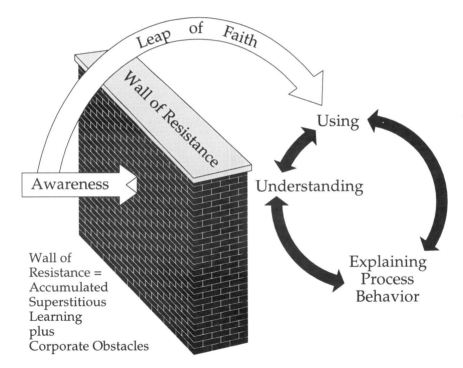

Figure 6.11: The Leap of Faith

---

14   Ed Peterson first suggested the leap of faith diagram to the author.

WHAT SHOULD YOU DO STARTING TOMORROW?

1. **Write out a list of the measures that you routinely see.**
    What kinds of data do you have at your disposal?

2. **Out of the list above, identify those measures that you use.**
    Some measures will be reported for your information, other measures will be the numbers that you actually use.

3. **Pick two or three measures that you actually use and start to plot them on a process behavior chart.**
    You may begin these charts with the current values, or you may go back and use historical values to get started. Either way, use the chart to learn what the voice of your current process may be. You have to begin charting something in order to practice the way of thinking that is part of this whole approach to understanding variation.

4. **Ask yourself if you are collecting the right data.**
    Both the data you collect and the data you report need to be useful, correct, and undistorted by artificial boundaries. Data which describe the activity are better than data which describe side effects of the process. Likewise, data which concern those things which the manager can control are more useful than mere report card data.

5. **Insist upon interpreting data within their context.**
    This will immediately require, among other things, a transformation of the monthly management report.

6. **Filter out the noise of routine variation before interpreting any value as a potential signal of exceptional variation.**
    The failure to do so is a mark of numerical naiveté, and the naive are fair game for the con artists.

7. **Cease to ask for explanations of noise.**
    In the absence of an identifiable signal, the current value cannot be said to differ from the preceding values. In the absence of a detectable signal no amount of explanation, however well worded and reasoned, can be supported by the data.

8. **Understand that no matter how the results may stack up against the specifications, a process which is predictable is performing as consistently as it possibly can in its current configuration.**
    For more about this see "If It Ain't Broke, Don't Fix It" in the appendices.

9. **Always distinguish between the Voice of the Process and the Voice of the Customer.**
    You cannot begin to get these two voices into alignment until you understand how they differ.

10. **Help others take action on assignable causes.**
    Knowing the assignable cause is only the first step. Detrimental assignable causes need to be eliminated. Beneficial ones need to be made part of the process.

BUT IT CAN'T BE THAT EASY, CAN IT?

Yes, it can.

One company had a monthly production meeting. Several managers would get together each month, review the figures, and plan the production schedule for the next month. Half of these managers had to fly from one location to another for this meeting. Between the meeting itself, the preparation time for those on site, and the travel time for the others, this meeting took over one full day out of the month for each manager who attended.

As the production personnel got more familiar with process behavior charts, the production manager began to plot the figures for the monthly production meeting on charts. As the group of managers got comfortable with the process behavior charts, and came to understand them, they quit reacting to routine monthly variation as if each swing was a signal. As they ceased to tamper with the process, the meeting started to get shorter. Finally, they no longer needed to have a face-to-face meeting. The discussion needed to set the production plan for the next month could now be handled with a conference call. Of course, the conference call represented a significant savings in time and money for all concerned.

After about a year of the conference calls, the group was sufficiently comfortable to shift to the use of e-mail to develop the monthly plan. This change represented a further savings in time for virtually all of the managers involved. Together, these changes essentially gave each manager an extra day each month!

The breakthrough for this group was the graphic presentation of their data and the application of the statistical thinking which is part and parcel of the process behavior chart.

Some seem to think that the solution to their problems couldn't be this simple. Well, it is and it isn't. The actual technique, the computations and the graphs are quite simple indeed. The way of thinking—the understanding of variation which motivates the technique and energizes the interpretation of the results—has to be cultivated. This will take both *time* and *practice*. There is no instant pudding. There is no shortcut.

Millions of people have proven, by their own experience, over the past 60 years, that process behavior charts work. This approach to understanding and using data is not on trial. The question is *not* whether or not the techniques will work—but rather whether or not *you* will make them work.

There's nothing to it but to do it.

> Those who *do not use process behavior charts*
> have no advantage over those who *can't*.

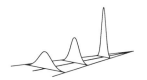

APPENDICES

THREE TYPES OF ACTION

1. Specifications
        are for taking action on the process outcomes—
            to separate the acceptable outcomes
                from the unacceptable outcomes
                    after the fact...
                        the Voice of the Customer.

2. Process Behavior Charts
        are for taking action on the process—
            to look for assignable causes of exceptional variation
                when they are present,
                    with an eye toward process improvement,
            and to refrain from looking for assignable causes
                when they are absent...
                    the Voice of the Process.

3. Actions to Align the Two Voices
        are appropriate—
            while this has been tried in the past,
                the lack of a well-defined Voice of the Process
                    has made alignment difficult to achieve.

A CHARACTERIZATION OF A PREDICTABLE PROCESS

1. When a process is predictable the variation in the process outcomes, or products, will be essentially the same day after day.

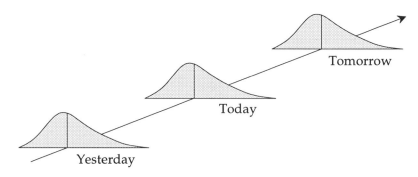

Figure A.1: The Past Predicts the Future

2. When a process is predictable we can find Natural Process Limits which will bracket virtually all of the process outcomes. These limits may be considered to be the Voice of the Process.

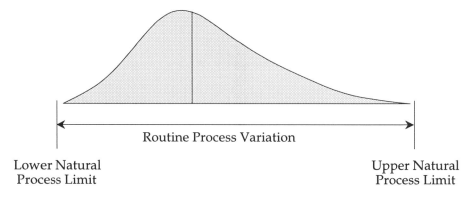

Figure A.2: The Natural Process Limits

3. If the Voice of the Process is not properly aligned with the Voice of the Customer, then some fraction of the product or outcomes will be nonconforming. While the observed fraction nonconforming may change from day to day, the basic fraction nonconforming will persist week to week or month to month.

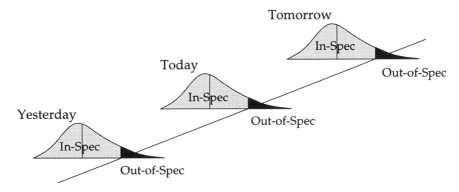

Figure A.3: Misalignment Between Voice of Process and Voice of Customer

4. When a process is predictable all of the outcomes are consequences of the common causes of routine variation. Seeking a special explanation for the existence of any outcomes that may be unacceptable will be a waste of time.

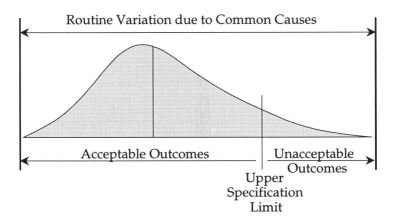

Figure A.4: Routine Variation Can Generate Both Good and Bad Product

5. When a process is predictable the only way to tackle the problem of unacceptable outcomes is to work to bring the voices into alignment. Either the process will have to be modified, or the specifications will have to be changed.

Either Shift the Process Aim:

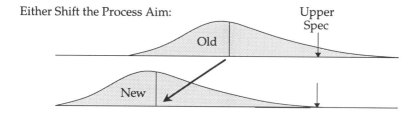

Or Reduce the Process Variation:

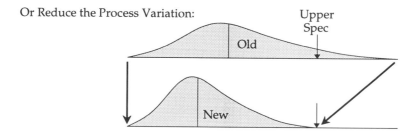

Or Change the Specs:

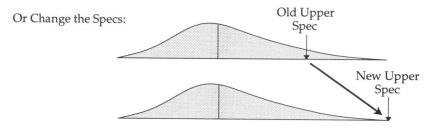

Figure A.5: Aligning the Voices

6. When a process is predictable the outcomes will vary within the Natural Process Limits—without regard for the Specification Limits.

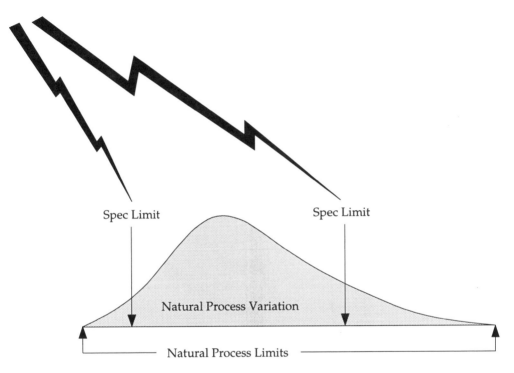

**Figure A.6: No Matter What the Specifications—
The Process Can Do No Better Than
The Voice of the Process**

A CHARACTERIZATION OF
AN UNPREDICTABLE PROCESS

1. An unpredictable process will display both routine variation and exceptional variation. The routine variation will be due to common causes, but the exceptional variation will be attributed to assignable causes. Since assignable causes will, by their very nature, dominate the common causes, the exceptional variation will dominate the routine variation and the process will behave unpredictably.

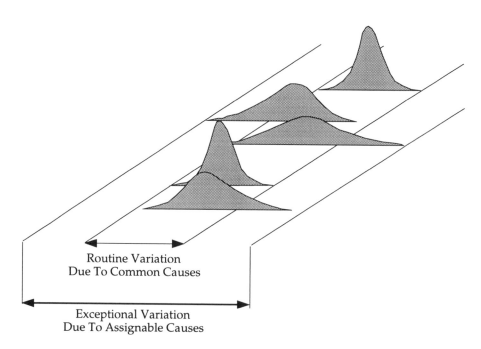

Routine Variation
Due To Common Causes

Exceptional Variation
Due To Assignable Causes

Figure A.7: An Unpredictable Process

2. Even if the past production has been 100 percent conforming, an unpredictable process will defy all of our attempts to characterize the future outcomes. The data shown below came from an unpredictable production process.

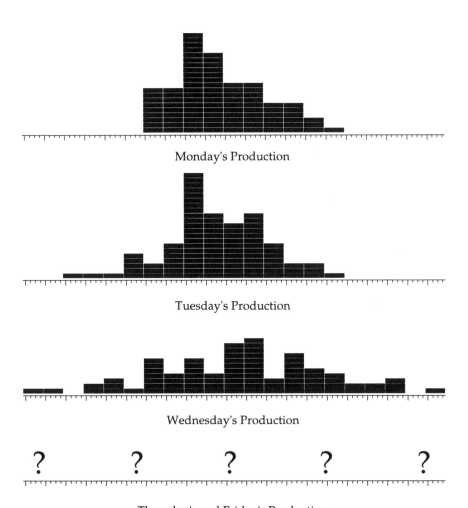

Figure A.8: One Week's Worth of Production

3. When a process is unpredictable the process behavior chart will detect the presence of the assignable causes. Each and every signal on a process behavior chart represents an opportunity to gain more insight into your process.

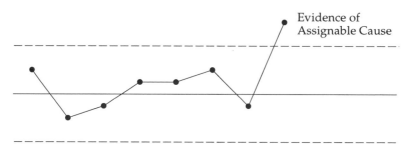

Figure A.9: Points Outside the Limits Are Signals

4. Shewhart constructed the process behavior chart in such a way that it will almost always be economical to spend the time to identify the assignable causes associated with the points outside the limits.

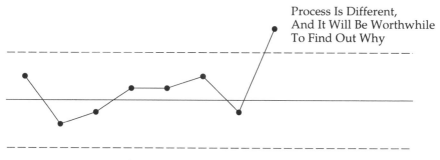

Figure A.10: Is Anybody Listening?

5. When a process is unpredictable, the outcomes will vary without regard for either the Natural Process Limits or the Specification Limits.

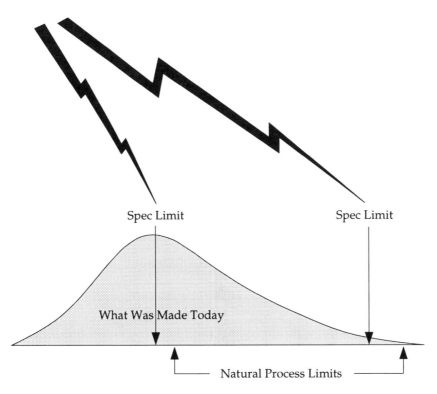

Figure A.11: When the Process is Unpredictable
About the Best You Can Say is
"Tomorrow Is Another Day"

FOR FURTHER READING

The Deming Dimension
by Henry Neave

A first-rate historical perspective which also clearly explains the tenets of the Deming philosophy. This book teaches us the answers that we need so that our hard work and best efforts may be rewarded with success rather than disappointment.

SPC Press, Knoxville, Tennessee

Fourth Generation Management: The New Business Consciousness
by Brian L. Joiner

How the evolution in management and the revolution in quality are converging and what it means for business and the nation. Required reading.

McGraw-Hill, New York

SPC at the Esquire Club
by Donald J. Wheeler

How a group of workers in a nightclub used the simple tools to improve service, reduce losses, and increase profits. Yes, it really can be this simple.

SPC Press, Knoxville, Tennessee

Deming Management at Work
by Mary Walton

Practical applications of the Deming management method in firms from all over the industrial spectrum.

The Putnam Publishing Group, New York

Out of the Crisis
by W. Edwards Deming

The source book for Dr. Deming's philosophy. Best when read in conjunction with *The Deming Dimension.*

MIT CAES Press, Cambridge, Mass.

Building Continual Improvement
by Donald J. Wheeler and Sheila R. Poling

This book was written as a sequel to *Understanding Variation, the Key to Managing Chaos*. It fills in the details that are needed for continual improvement in the service industry and the administrative areas of your organization.

SPC Press, Knoxville, Tennessee

Understanding Statistical Process Control, Second Edition
by Donald J. Wheeler and David S. Chambers

Voted "One of the ten top books on quality." This textbook is the new standard reference for those who want to read more about Dr. Shewhart's techniques. This text clearly explains both the tools and the philosophy using manufacturing and process industry examples.

SPC Press, Knoxville, Tennessee

Deming's Road to Continual Improvement
by William W. Scherkenbach

Understanding Profound Knowledge involves a revolution in thought. Operationalizing Profound Knowledge requires an evolution in practice. Both of these requirements are addressed in this unique book. It shows how these concepts can be put to work in your business.

SPC Press, Knoxville, Tennessee

The New Economics
by W. Edwards Deming

This is Dr. Deming's sequel to *Out of the Crisis*. Best when read after *The Deming Dimension* and *Out of the Crisis*.

MIT CAES Press, Cambridge, Mass.

The Improvement Guide
by Gerald J. Langley, Kevin M. Nolan, Thomas W. Nolan,
Clifford L. Norman, and Lloyd P. Provost

A valuable source book for the nuts and bolts of continual improvement via the Plan, Do, Study, Act cycle.

Jossey-Bass Publishers, San Francisco

XMR CHARTS USING THE MEDIAN MOVING RANGE

- Use the individual values to compute the *Average*, $\overline{X}$.
  This value will be the central line for the X chart.[15]

- Find the moving ranges and
  obtain the ***Median Moving Range***, $\widetilde{mR}$.
  This value will be the central line for the mR chart.

- To find the **Upper Natural Process Limit** for the X chart:
  multiply the ***Median Moving Range*** by 3.14
  and add the product to the ***Average***. [15]

$$UNPL = \overline{X} + (3.14 \times \widetilde{mR})$$

- To find the **Lower Natural Process Limit** for the X chart:
  multiply the ***Median Moving Range*** by 3.14
  and subtract the product from the ***Average***. [15]

$$LNPL = \overline{X} - (3.14 \times \widetilde{mR})$$

- To find the **Upper Range Limit** for the mR Chart:
  multiply the ***Median Moving Range*** by 3.87.

$$URL = 3.87 \times \widetilde{mR}$$

The multiplicative constants of 3.14 and 3.87 seen in the equations above are the scaling factors needed to convert the median moving range so you can obtain the appropriate limits on each portion of the chart.

---

[15] In these computations the *Median of the Individual Values* may be used in place of the *Average of the Individual Values*.

XMR CHARTS USING THE AVERAGE MOVING RANGE

- Use the individual values to compute the *Average*, $\overline{X}$.
    This value will be the central line for the X chart.

- Find the moving ranges and
    compute the *Average Moving Range, $\overline{mR}$* .
        This value will be the central line for the mR chart.

- To find the **Upper Natural Process Limit** for the X chart:
    multiply the *Average Moving Range* by 2.66
        and add the product to the *Average*.

$$ UNPL = \overline{X} + (2.66 \times \overline{mR}) $$

- To find the **Lower Natural Process Limit** for the X chart:
    multiply the *Average Moving Range* by 2.66
        and subtract the product from the *Average*.

$$ LNPL = \overline{X} - (2.66 \times \overline{mR}) $$

- To find the **Upper Range Limit** for the mR chart:
    multiply the *Average Moving Range* by 3.27.

$$ URL = 3.27 \times \overline{mR} $$

The multiplicative constants of 2.66 and 3.27 seen in the equations above are the scaling factors needed to convert the Average Moving Range so you can obtain the appropriate limits on each portion of the chart.

WHY NOT USE P - CHARTS ?

Many would be tempted to use a *p*-chart with the on-time shipment data on pages 45–48, with the premium freight shipment data on pages 49–52, and with the on-time closing data on pages 82–83. However, in each case there is a problem with doing so—namely, the assumptions of the binomial probability model are not satisfied. In particular, the probability of a shipment being on time *is not constant for all the shipments in any given month*; the probability of a shipment being shipped by air *is not constant for all the shipments in any given month*; and the probability of a department's books being closed on time *is not constant for all 35 departments in any given month*. This variable likelihood (within each time-period) for the occurrence of the attribute being counted will, in each case, undermine the use of the binomial probability model and will make the *p*-chart limits incorrect and inappropriate.

When can you use a *p*-chart or an *np*-chart? Only when the binomial probability model is appropriate. When can you use a *c*-chart or a *u*-chart? Only when the Poisson probability model is appropriate. If you do not know how to evaluate the appropriateness of the binomial probability model and the Poisson probability model, then you should avoid using the specialized charts that are based on these models.

When can you use an *XmR* chart with count based data? Anytime you wish. Since the *np*-chart, the *p*-chart, the *c*-chart, and the *u*-chart are all special cases of the chart for individual values, the *XmR* chart will mimic these specialized charts when they would be appropriate. However, when the specialized charts are inappropriate, the *XmR* chart will still work because it uses an empirical approach rather than being based on a specific probability model. Therefore, if you do not know how to verify a particular probability model, or do not care to do so, you can still use an *XmR* chart with your count-based data.

A MODEST PROPOSAL

The body of techniques commonly known as Statistical Process Control have been around for over 70 years. However, from the very beginning, and continuing down to the present, there has been considerable confusion about the nature and purpose of SPC. I believe this is because many have sought to reshape SPC according to their own background and experience.

Some hear the words Statistical Process Control and immediately think of classical statistical procedures. They try to fit SPC into this framework of mathematical models, probability distributions, estimates of parameters, tests of hypotheses, and confidence levels. Of course, when this group tries to share their version of SPC they are met with that same total lack of comprehension which is the fate of classical statistics. But statisticians are accustomed to rejection, so this is nothing new.

Others hear the words Statistical Process Control and mentally insert a hyphen between the last two words—SPC is thought of as a manual technique for "process-*hyphen*-control." The objective is to maintain the *status quo* for a process. It is merely a process-monitoring technique; something to be used after you have already gotten the process into a satisfactory state. "And, since this is what SPC is about, wouldn't you like to know about some of the neat algorithmic process-control techniques and process-modeling techniques that have been developed in the past few years?" This group would be glad to enroll you in a seminar or sell you some software. But once again, there is a hurdle of truly mathematical proportions to be overcome. The faint of heart need not apply. Those without calculus should not enter into this door.

A third group uses the word "control" to denote conformance to specifications, and so when they hear the words Statistical Process Control they think about trying to produce product within specifications. Given this perspective, they think of SPC as a complex route to a simple objective, and accordingly they try to simplify SPC. This group tends to want to bypass the computations based on the data and instead use the specifications to set action limits. While this simplicity sells well, it has the unfortunate characteristic of completely misrepresenting what SPC is all about. Those who use these simplified approaches may meet with some limited success, but because their objective falls short of what can be done, because they do not seek to get the most out of their processes, they do not reap the benefits available from SPC. The reality falls short of the promise, and the users return to sorting as a way of life—make enough stuff and some of it is likely to be good.

And then there is the group that is confused by the three groups above. They do not understand the first two interpretations of SPC, but they presume that there must be something to all the mathematics, and so they encumber SPC with all sorts of distributional assumptions, cautions, and requirements. These superstitious restrictions on how and when to use SPC become obstacles and impediments that discourage all but the most determined users.

Enough of this nonsense! Statistical Process Control is not about statistics, it is not about "process-hyphen-control," and it is not about conformance to specifications. While SPC can be used in all of these ways, it is much more than any one of these narrow interpretations. It is, at its heart, about getting the most from your processes. It is about the continual improvement of processes and outcomes. And it is, first and foremost, *a way of thinking* with some tools attached.

While it is easy to focus on the tools, and while it is easy to teach the tools, the tools are secondary to the way of thinking. Learn the tools and you will have nothing. You will not know what to do. You will not know how to use the tools effectively.

Learn and practice the way of thinking that undergirds the tools and you will begin an unending journey of continual improvement. Without major capital expenditures you will discover how to increase both quality and productivity, and thereby to improve your competitive position.

This is not a theory. This has been proven time after time. But of course, the successful companies are reluctant to share this secret with their competitors (even if their competitors could understand it).

And this is where the nomenclature gets in the way. As outlined above, as long as we use the words Statistical Process Control we will stimulate people to think about techniques for maintaining the *status quo*. As long as we talk about "control charts" we will continue to be misunderstood as described above simply because of the many different connotations of the word control. The words "out of control" will generally bring to mind the image of a disgruntled worker going crazy and shooting his fellow workers. On the other hand, the words "in control" are used to mean "under my control" and "in specification."

So, to understand just what Shewhart meant when he used the word "control," we turn to his own definition:

"A phenomenon will be said to be controlled when,
through the use of past experience,
we can predict, at least within limits,
how the phenomenon will vary in the future."

Here we see that *predictability* is the essence of Shewhart's use of the word control. A phenomenon that is controlled is predictable, and conversely, a phenomenon that is not controlled is unpredictable. Consider how the sense of Shewhart's definition is unchanged by the following paraphrase:

A *process* will be said to be *predictable* when,
through the use of past experience,
we can *describe*, at least within limits,
how the *process* will *behave* in the future.

The substitution of these four words does not change the thrust of Shewhart's idea, but it does avoid some of the confusion that his original words have engendered.

Thus, the control chart is, in effect, a *process behavior chart*. It examines the data from a process to see if the process is *predictable* or *unpre-*

dictable. When a process is unpredictable it will display the *exceptional variation* that is the result of assignable causes. When a process is predictable it will display the *routine variation* that is characteristic of common causes.

Therefore, in order to better win the hearts and minds of others, and to encourage them to enjoy the benefits of Shewhart's creation, consider using the following terminology.

Instead of Statistical Process Control,
talk about Methods of Continual Improvement.

This has the advantage of focusing attention on the job of making things better by getting the most out of our current systems and processes as opposed to merely monitoring the process to maintain the *status quo.*

Instead of control charts,
talk about process behavior charts.

This has the advantage of avoiding the baggage associated with the word "control" while correctly describing how to use the chart to get the most out of an existing process.

Instead of an in-control process,
talk about a predictable process.

Instead of an out-of-control process,
talk about an unpredictable process.

All too often the words "in-control" are used to describe a situation where all of the product falls within the specification limits. The words "predictable" and "unpredictable" do not carry the same connotations. It is easy to make a distinction between a "predictable process" and "acceptable product."

Instead of an out-of-control point,
talk about a point outside the limits.

Instead of an in-control point,
talk about a point inside the limits.

This simply replaces emotionally loaded terms with descriptive phrases.

Instead of control limits for individual values,
talk about natural process limits.

Instead of control limits for averages,
talk about limits for averages
(Upper Average Limit, Lower Average Limit).

Instead of control limits for ranges,
talk about limits for ranges
(Upper Range Limit, Lower Range Limit).

These changes are not as hard to get used to as they might seem at first, and they avoid the red-herring of "control limits."

Finally, I must acknowledge that the idea of a better terminology is not mine alone. Process behavior charts came from Dr. Sophronia Ward. Natural process limits came from Professor David S. Chambers. Predictable and unpredictable was the suggestion of Mike Kazeef.

After years of working for a better understanding using the traditional terminology, I have finally come to the point that I am convinced that a new terminology is necessary to clearly and effectively communicate the purpose and use of the powerful techniques of Continual Improvement.

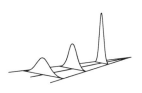

IF IT AIN'T BROKE, DON'T FIX IT

For many hundreds of years the phrase *if it ain't broke, don't fix it* has summarized the predominant approach to process operation. From the physician's admonition to *do no harm*, to the slightly more positive aphorism *the squeaky wheel gets the grease* there is a common theme of differentiating between those things that need to be attended to and those that do not. When your process is in trouble, then you should do something about that trouble, but when your process is operating okay, then leave it alone—and every process can be characterized as either being in trouble or as operating okay.

Trouble is usually fairly easy to identify. A piece of equipment is in trouble when it ceases to operate. With a production process, trouble may be defined by too much nonconforming product. With a service process, trouble may consist of too many complaints, or a rework rate that is too high. Whatever the situation, trouble is whatever upsets the boss, and the absence of trouble is generally taken to be a sign that things are operating okay.

Figure A.12: The Traditional Definition of Trouble

Of course, whenever you are in trouble you will recognize the need to do something to alleviate the trouble—no one will argue against fixing a broken process. So don't just stand there, do something! Buy a new technology, undertake a major process upgrade, form a problem-solving team, or reengineer the process!

Thus, we have the squeaky wheel approach to process operation. It seeks relief when the trouble becomes intolerable, but otherwise it avoids rocking the boat as long as the process is thought to be operating okay. The squeaky wheel approach is driven by the unacceptable outcomes, and ultimately, it is based on a pessimistic view of the effects of your intervention—you could make things worse, so wait until the outcomes are so bad that anything you do will constitute an improvement.

Eventually you may get beyond this; you may develop enough expertise in operating your own process that you will feel comfortable in trying to improve your process even before it is in trouble. When this happens you will get to the point of tweaking your process even when it is operating okay. Thus, we could express the sum of centuries of conventional wisdom as:

Ignore (or tweak) the good processes,
and reengineer the bad processes.

This statement summarizes the traditional approach to process management.

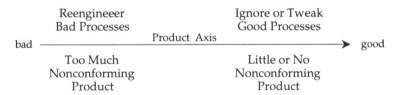

Figure A.13: Squeaky Wheel Improvement

While this traditional approach does pay heed to the scrap rate, it does not incorporate the effects of variation. And the effects of variation lead to a second definition of what constitutes trouble; a definition that is based upon the way the process behaves over time. In particular, it turns out that the behavior of every process can be characterized as being either predictable (within limits) or unpredictable.

When your process is predictable you may use the past as a guide to the future. While you may not be able to predict specific future values, you can describe the range of routine values to be expected in the future. And since the essence of management is prediction, the benefits of having a predictable process are manifold. In addition, a predictable process is one that is operating up to its potential—it will be operating with maximum consistency and minimum variation. Clearly it is good to have this type of process.

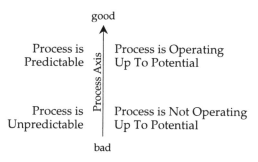

Figure A.14: The New Definition of Trouble

On the other hand, an unpredictable process will not be operating up to its full potential: it will not be operating with maximum consistency, it will not be operating with minimum variation, and it will be subject to unpredictable changes. Clearly an unpredictable process will create many headaches. However, an unpredictable process will always contain clues about what is causing the excessive variation and the unpredictable changes.

When you learn how to use process behavior charts to detect these clues, and when as a result of this knowledge you take actions to remove the effects of these causes from your process, then you will improve both the predictability of your process and the consistency of your process outcomes.

While both predictable and unpredictable processes are described more completely in this book, we are concerned here with the implications for improvement that arise from this distinction. When a process is predictable it cannot be improved by simple tweaking. Since a predictable process is operating at full potential, you can only improve it by changing it in some fundamental manner. This might be a new system, or a new technology, or new process settings, or new ways of doing the work. But it will always require changing the process in some major way.

However, when a process is unpredictable it is not operating up to its potential because it is subject to the effects of assignable causes of exceptional variation. By finding and removing the effects of these assignable causes you can substantially improve both process consistency and process outcomes. In short, you can begin to get your process to operate up to its potential. It is not a matter of capital expenditures or process upgrades, but merely a matter of tweaking the existing process by identifying the causes of unpredictable variation and removing their effects.

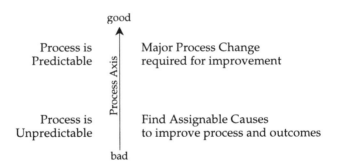

Figure A.15: The Implications of Process Behavior

Thus, if we define a predictable process as a good process, and an unpredictable process as a bad process, we could summarize the consequences of the new definition of trouble as:

Reengineer the good processes,
and tweak the bad processes;

which is exactly the opposite of the traditional view summarized earlier!

So while the squeaky wheel approach and process-based improvement seem to give contradictory advice on how to "fix it," the complete picture can only be found by combining these two definitions of trouble. Since these two definitions are independent of each other we will have to represent them using two different axes on a graph. On the horizontal axis we will place the traditional definition, while the new definition will be placed on the vertical axis. When we do this we end up with four possibilities which can be used to characterize every process.

No Trouble: A process could be *predictable* while producing *little or no nonconforming product.*

Trouble Old Style: A process could be *predictable* while producing *too much nonconforming product.*

Trouble New Style: A process could be *unpredictable* while producing *little or no nonconforming product.*

Double Trouble: A process could be *unpredictable* while producing *too much nonconforming product.*

Since these four possibilities represent reality, every realistic apprasial of a situation will require the use of these four categories. This combination of the two definitions of trouble leads to an understanding that an unpredictable process is in trouble regardless of the level of nonconforming product. And this, in turn, has implications regarding the maintenance and improvement of your processes.

If you have a process in the No Trouble State, then indeed, you might well leave it alone. The outcomes are acceptable, and the process is operating up to its full potential. You and your customer are getting what you paid for.

If you have a process that is characterized by Trouble Old Style, you will have external pressure to improve your process outcomes. However, the fact that your process is operating predictably means that it is operating at its full potential—it is doing the best it can do. Therefore, you will need to change this process in some fundamental manner. So, go ahead and buy a new technology, undertake a major process upgrade, form a

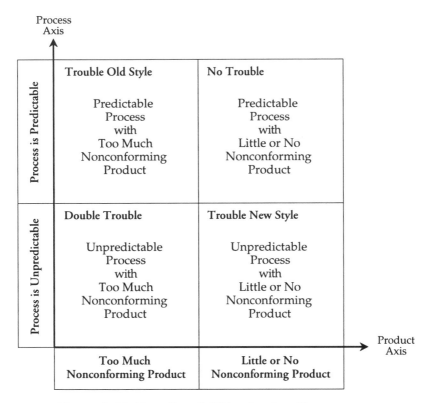

Figure A.16: Four Possibilities for Any Process

problem-solving team, or reengineer the process.

Thus, we see that the traditional view is appropriate when you have a predictable process:

Ignore (or tweak) the good predictable processes,
and reengineer the bad predictable processes.

But what about processes in the other two categories? If you have a process that is characterized by Trouble New Style, or is in Double Trouble, then you have a process that is unpredictable. Regardless of the suitability of the process outcomes, the unpredictability of the process will undermine all the predictions and all the process modifications that you may try to make. Moreover, when your process is unpredictable it is not operating up to its full potential. Therefore, by finding the causes of the unpredictable variation, and by removing their effects from your process, you can, with virtually no capital expense, improve both your process and your process outcomes. Since finding and removing assignable causes is generally much easier and cheaper than performing a major process upgrade, this approach should always be the first one to use with an unpredictable process. Therefore:

> *When a process displays unpredictable behavior,*
> *you can most easily improve the process and process outcomes*
> *by identifying the assignable causes of unpredictable variation*
> *and removing their effects from your process.*

"Why should I try to improve a bad process? Couldn't I just completely replace the unpredictable process with a new process?"

Yes, you could. But it will cost less to find the assignable causes and remove their effects. Moreover, replacing an unpredictable process with a new process will, in the end, merely replace old problems with new problems. After all, you know from your own experience that new processes rarely work as well as they are supposed to work. The reason for this is simple—if you cannot operate your current process predictably, what makes you think that you can operate a new process predictably? If you are not getting the most out of your current process it is unlikely that you will get the most out of a new process. So replacing an unpredictable process with a new process will usually end up as a case of "out of the frying pan, into the fire."

Thus, when we combine the traditional *product*-based definition of trouble with the new *process*-based definition we obtain a more sophisticated description of our processes. These four possibilities outline a more realistic way of approaching the problems of repeatedly delivering a product or a service that will be of value to our customers. This more realistic, process-based approach to "when to fix it" allows you to take advantage

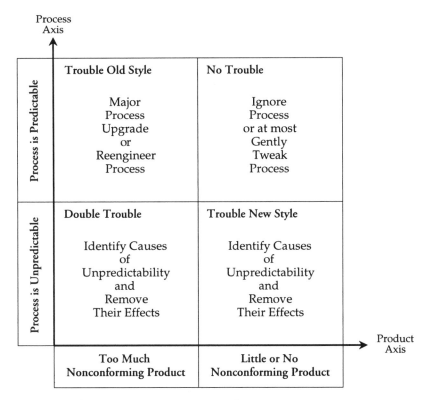

Figure A.17: Process-Based Improvement

of the quicker, cheaper solutions when they will work, and to know when more fundamental changes are required.

While the traditional squeaky wheel approach to process improvement will work when you have a predictable process, it can be a waste of time and money when you have an unpredictable process. And it is a fact of life that most of your production processes will be unpredictable. Predictable production processes are obtained, and then maintained, through the effective use of process behavior charts. They do not tend to occur naturally or spontaneously. This alone will make the process-based approach to improvement more reliable, and more sustainable, than any other approach you may try.

INDEX